ENDANGERED ANIMALS

COLORING BOOK

INTRODUCTION

Welcome to "Endangered Animals: Coloring Book" where creativity meets conservation. In this unique book, you will embark on a journey through the fascinating world of endangered species while unleashing your artistic talents through coloring.

Each page of this coloring book features stunning illustrations of endangered animals from around the globe, waiting for you to bring them to life with color. But this book is more than just a coloring adventure. It's also an educational tool filled with valuable information about each animal, including their threats and conservation efforts.

As you color, you'll learn about the challenges facing these magnificent creatures and the importance of protecting their habitats. From majestic tigers and gentle giant pandas to graceful sea turtles and majestic blue whales, each animal has its own story to tell, and by coloring their portraits, you become part of their journey toward survival.

Join us as we celebrate the beauty and diversity of our planet's wildlife and work together to ensure a future where these magnificent animals continue to thrive in the wild. So grab your colored pencils, markers, or crayons, and let's embark on an inspiring and colorful adventure to protect endangered animals for generations to come.

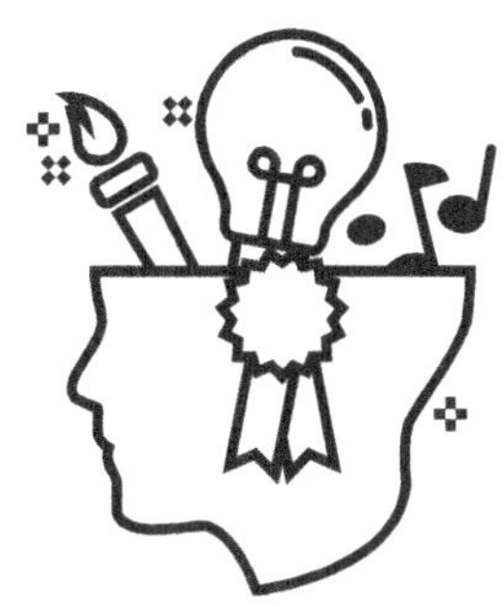

WRITE ME LIFESTYLE

No part of this book may be scanned, reproduced or distributed in any printed or electronic from without the prior permission of the author or publisher.

We love to receive reviews from our costumers. If you had the opportunity to provide a review we would greatly appreciate it.

THANK YOU!

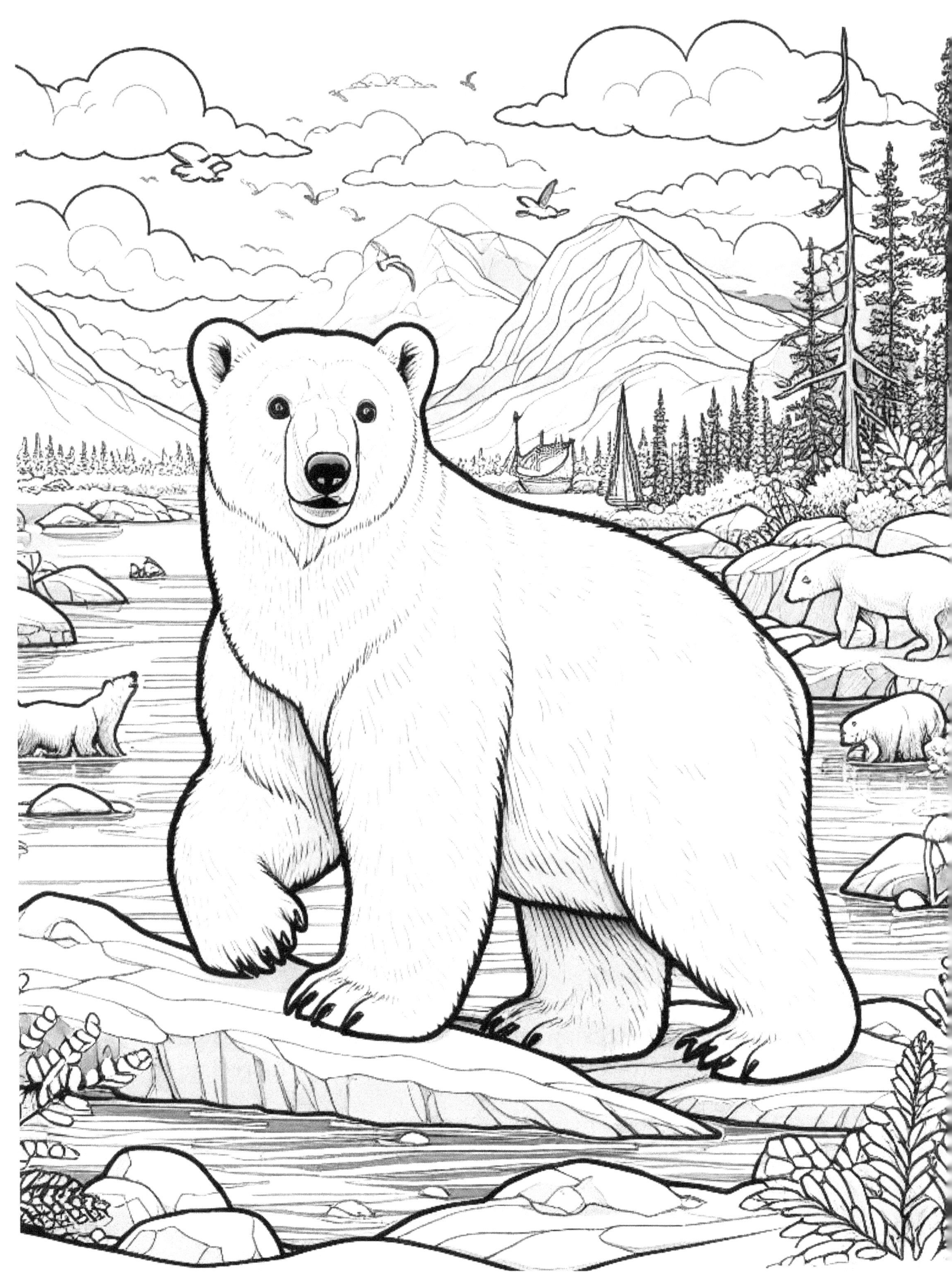

THE POLAR BEAR

The polar bear, is a species of carnivorous mammal that inhabits the Arctic regions of the world, especially within the Arctic Circle. They are famous for their distinctive white fur, which helps them blend into their icy environment, as well as their ability to survive in extremely cold conditions.

Why is the polar bear endangered?

Climate change and loss of sea ice are the main threats to polar bears, as they rely on ice for hunting and reproduction. Declining sea ice makes it harder for them to find food and can lead to increased conflicts with humans searching for food.

Conservation

The International Union for Conservation of Nature (IUCN) classifies the polar bear as "Vulnerable" due to population decline and habitat loss.

Conserving polar bears requires global efforts to address climate change, protect their habitat, and minimize conflicts with humans in areas where they interact.

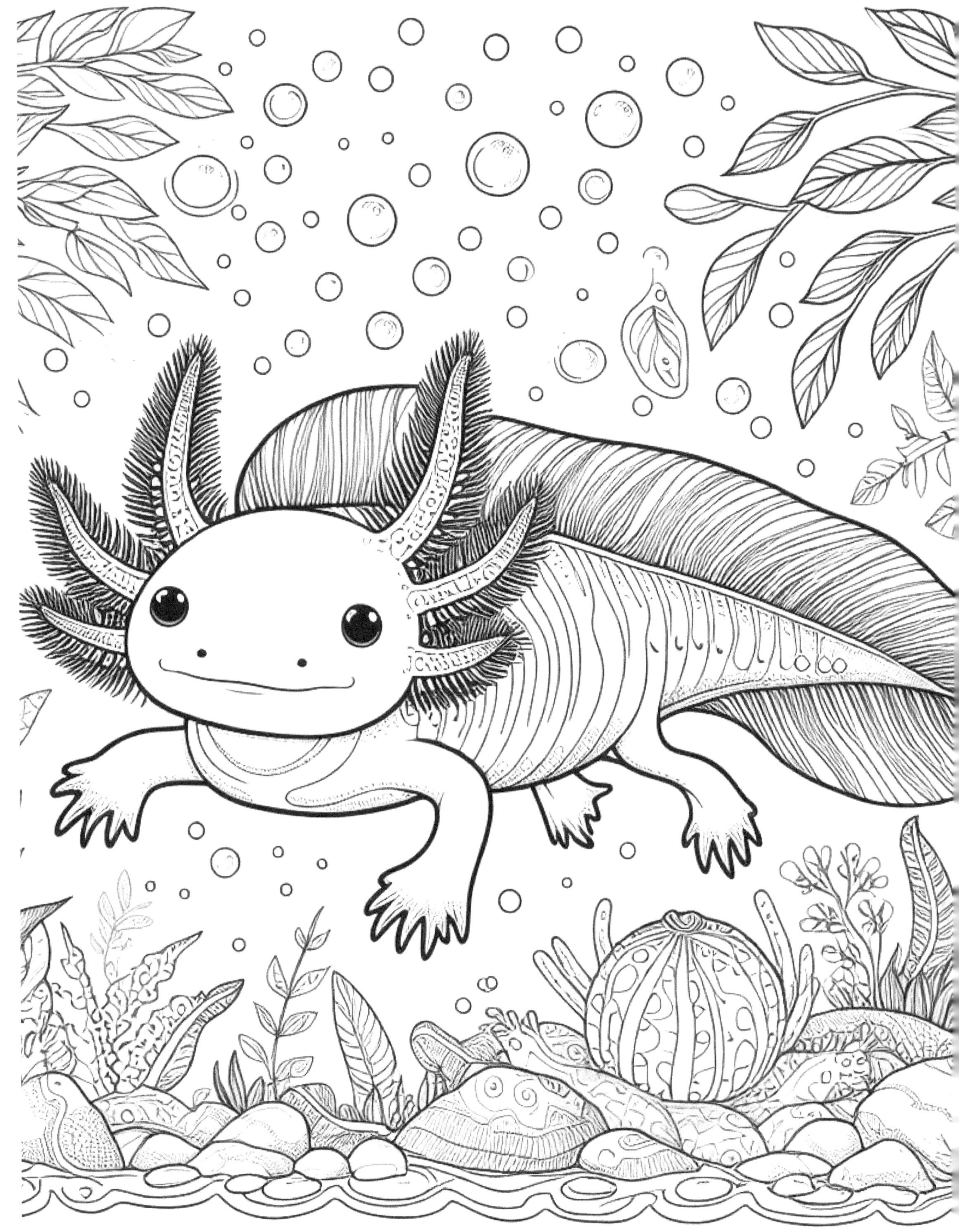

THE AXOLOTL

The axolotl, also known as Ambystoma mexicanum, is a species of salamander endemic to Mexico, specifically from the aquatic systems of Lake Xochimilco and Lake Chalco, as well as some surrounding areas in the Valley of Mexico. This fascinating creature is known for its unique ability to regenerate body parts, its neotenic appearance (retention of juvenile features into adulthood), and its cultural and scientific significance.

Why is the axolotl endangered?

the axolotl faces various threats, including habitat loss due to urbanization, water pollution, and the introduction of invasive species.

Conservation

Several conservation initiatives are working to protect the axolotl and its habitat, including the establishment of sanctuaries and captive breeding programs.

The axolotl is an emblematic symbol of Mexico's biodiversity and a remarkable example of the amazing adaptation and diversity of life on the planet. However, its survival is threatened, and ongoing efforts are needed to ensure its long-term conservation.

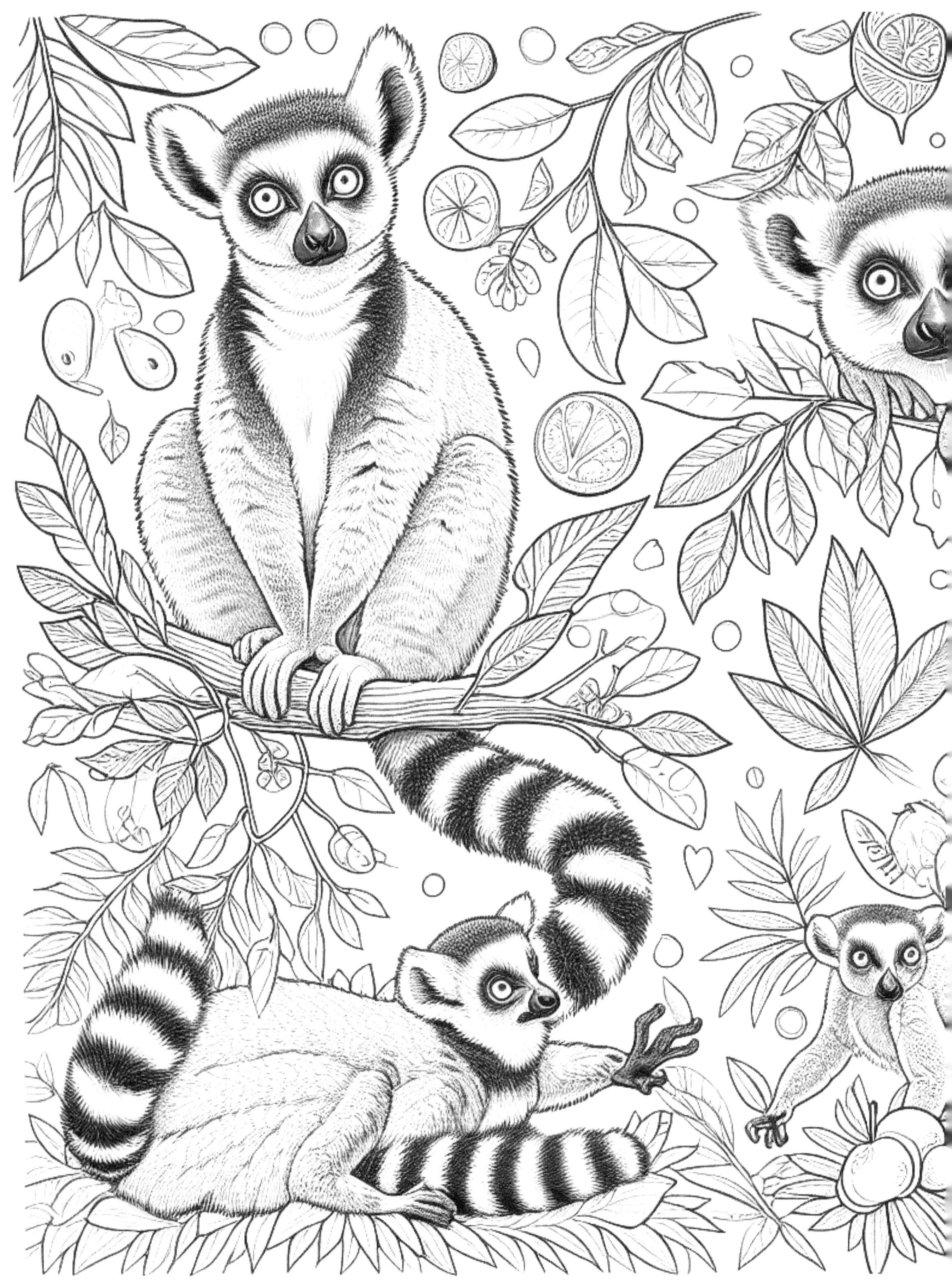

THE LEMUR

The lemur is a type of primate that is endemic to the island of Madagascar and the nearby Comoros Islands. Lemurs are known for their unique appearance, including their large, reflective eyes, furry bodies, and long tails. They come in a variety of sizes, ranging from the tiny mouse lemur to the larger indri. Lemurs are also known for their diverse behaviors and adaptations to different habitats within Madagascar, including rainforests, dry forests, and spiny forests.

Why is the the Lemur endangered?

Lemurs face numerous threats to their survival, including habitat destruction due to deforestation, slash-and-burn agriculture, and illegal logging. Additionally, lemurs are hunted for bushmeat, captured for the illegal pet trade, and threatened by climate change.

Conservation

Conservation organizations and researchers are working to protect lemurs and their habitats through various means, including habitat restoration, community-based conservation initiatives, ecotourism, and scientific research.

Importance to Ecosystem

Lemurs play a crucial role in Madagascar's ecosystems as seed dispersers, pollinators, and prey for predators. Their decline could have cascading effects on the health and stability of Madagascar's forests and biodiversity.

Overall, lemurs are iconic symbols of Madagascar's unique natural heritage, but they are also among the world's most endangered primates. Efforts to conserve lemurs and their habitats are critical for ensuring their survival and the preservation of Madagascar's extraordinary biodiversity.

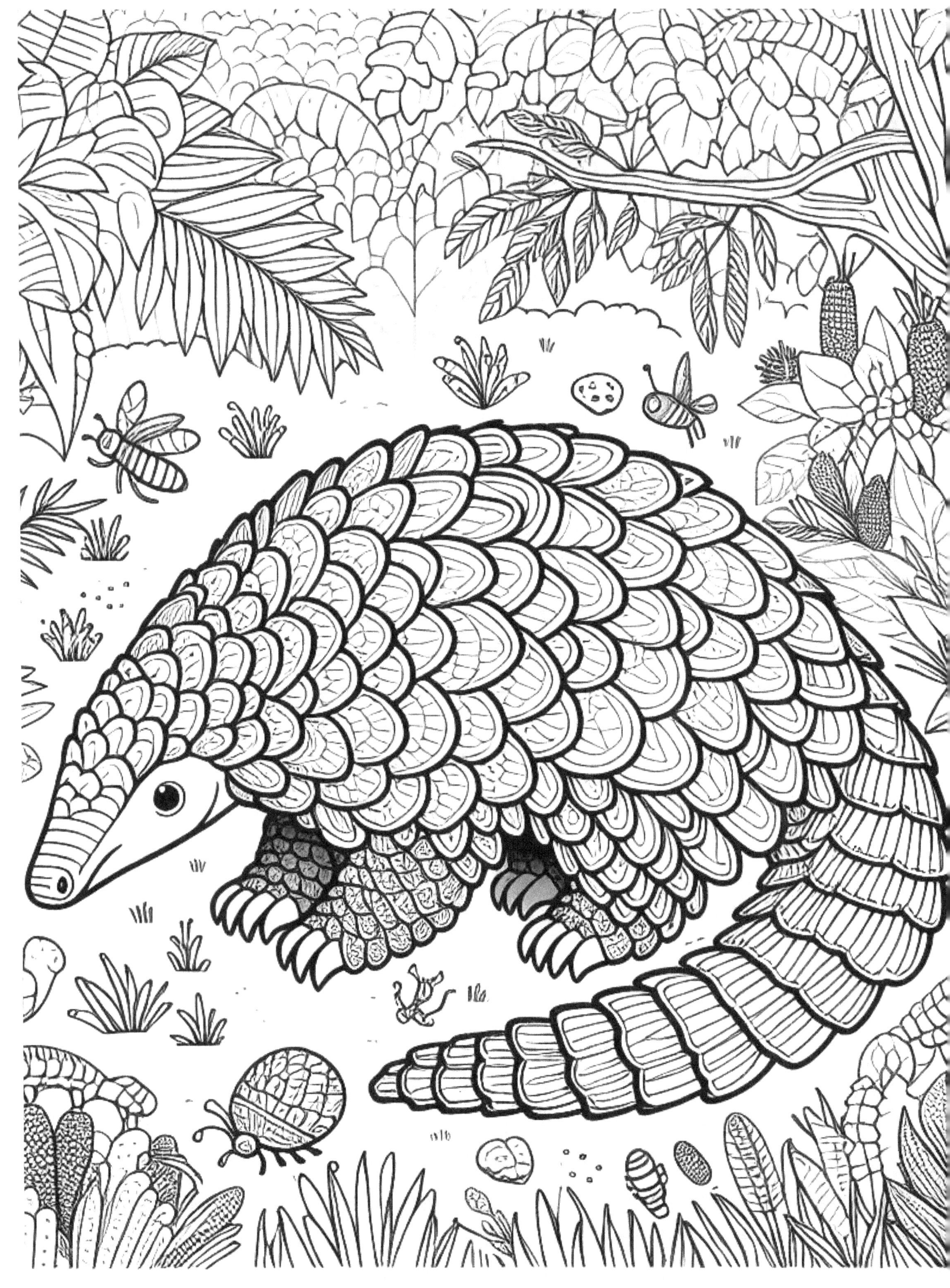

THE PANGOLIN

The pangolin is a scaly mammal belonging to the order Pholidota and the family Manidae. They are known for their distinctive covering of hard, sharp scales, which they use as protective armor against predators. There are eight species of pangolins, four of which are found in Africa and four in Asia.

Why is the Pangolin endangered?

Pangolins are one of the most trafficked species in the world due to the demand for their scales and meat in traditional Asian medicine, as well as their consideration as a delicacy in some countries. Poaching and illegal trade have led to a dramatic decline in pangolin populations worldwide.

Conservation

Conservation efforts are underway to protect pangolins and combat illegal trafficking. These include the implementation of stricter laws, strengthening law enforcement, public education, and promoting sustainable alternatives to pangolin products in traditional medicine.

In summary, the pangolin is a unique and fascinating species facing serious threats due to poaching and illegal trade. Protecting pangolins and their habitats is crucial to ensure their long-term survival and to maintain the balance of the ecosystems they inhabit.

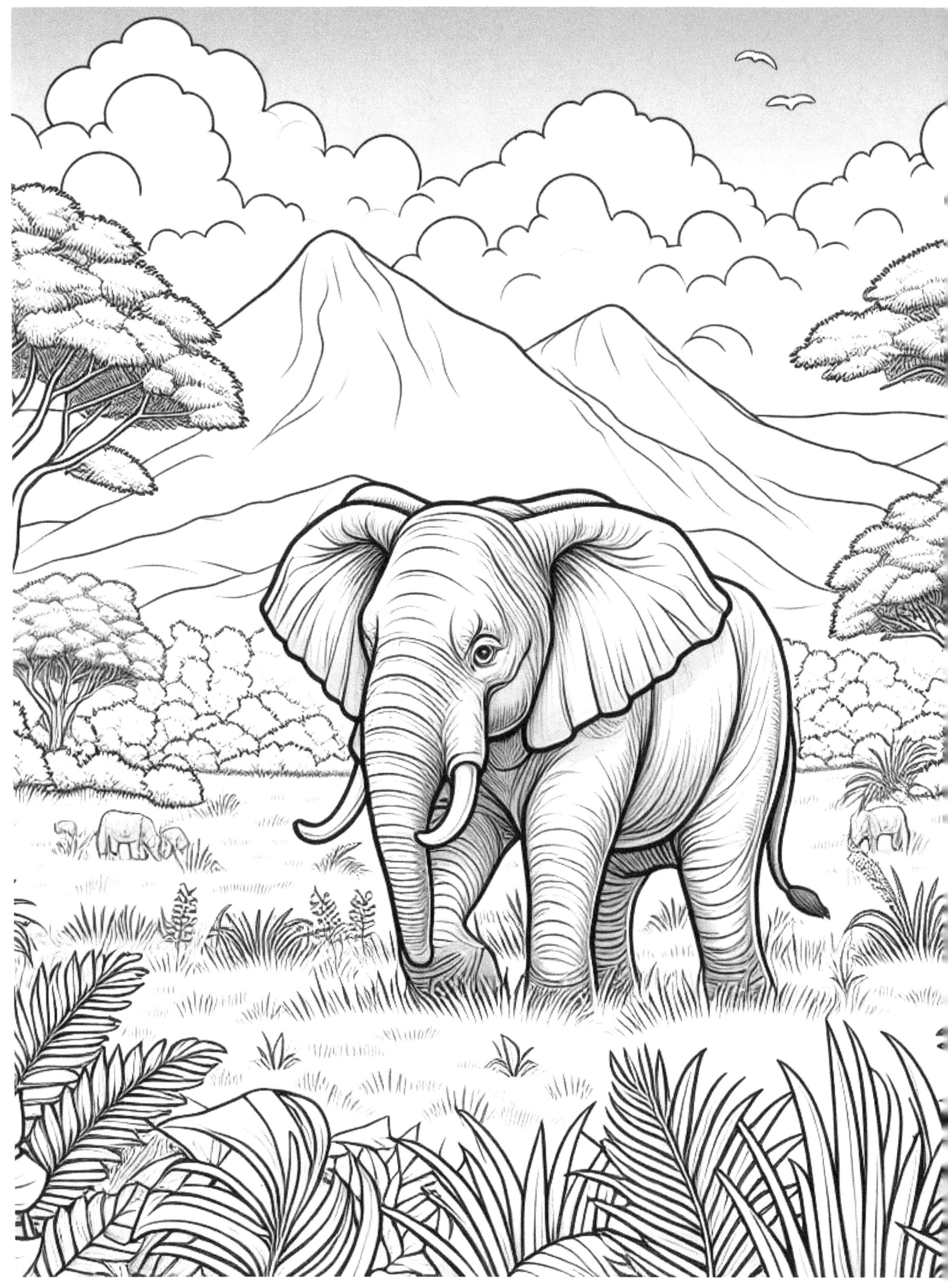

THE ASIAN ELEPHANT

The Asian elephant, also known as Elephas maximus, is one of the two species of elephants in the world, the other being the African elephant. They are impressive and iconic animals that inhabit various countries in Asia, including India, Sri Lanka, Thailand, Indonesia, among others.

Why is the Asian elephant endangered?

The Asian elephant faces numerous threats, including loss and degradation of habitat, poaching for ivory and meat, and conflict with humans due to competition for resources and crop destruction.

Conservation

Conservation efforts are underway to protect the Asian elephant, including the creation of protected areas, wildlife corridors, conflict mitigation programs, and public awareness campaigns. However, the situation of this species remains concerning, and ongoing commitment is needed to ensure its long-term survival.

In summary, the Asian elephant is an iconic and emblematic species of Asia facing serious threats due to habitat loss and poaching. Protecting these majestic animals is crucial for conserving the biodiversity of Asian ecosystems and ensuring their survival for future generations.

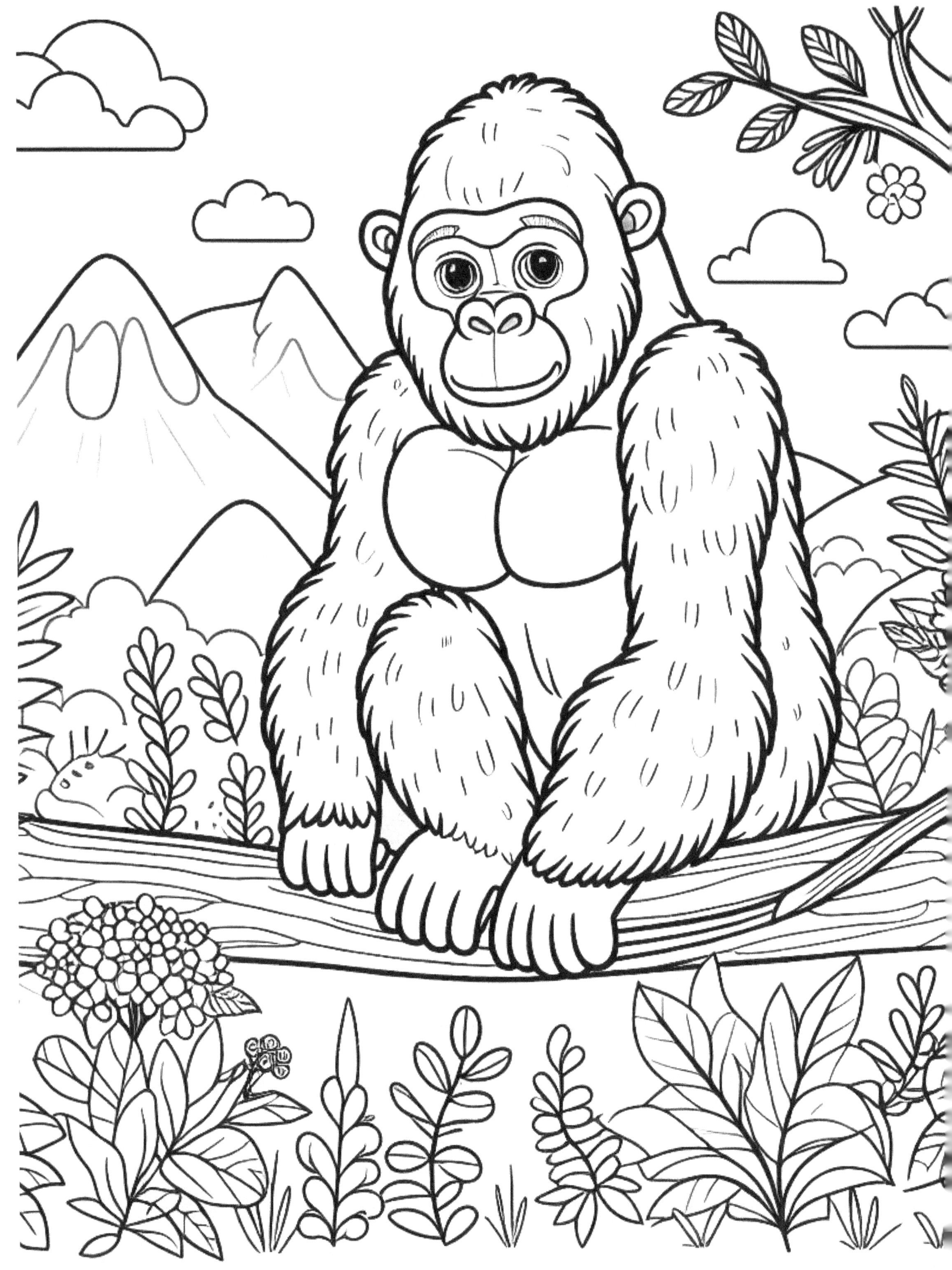

THE MOUNTAIN GORILLA

The mountain gorilla, is one of the most well-known and iconic subspecies of gorilla. These primates inhabit the mountains of Central Africa, specifically the montane forests and jungles of the Great Lakes region of Africa, which includes parts of Uganda, Rwanda, and the Democratic Republic of the Congo.

Why is the mountain gorilla endangered?

The mountain gorilla is listed as "Critically Endangered" on the IUCN Red List of Threatened Species, primarily due to poaching, habitat loss, and diseases transmitted by humans. However, conservation efforts, such as responsible ecotourism and protection of protected areas, have helped stabilize some populations.

In summary, the mountain gorilla is an iconic and emblematic species facing serious threats due to habitat loss and poaching. Protecting these magnificent primates is crucial for conserving the biodiversity of the mountain forests of Central Africa and ensuring their survival for future generations.

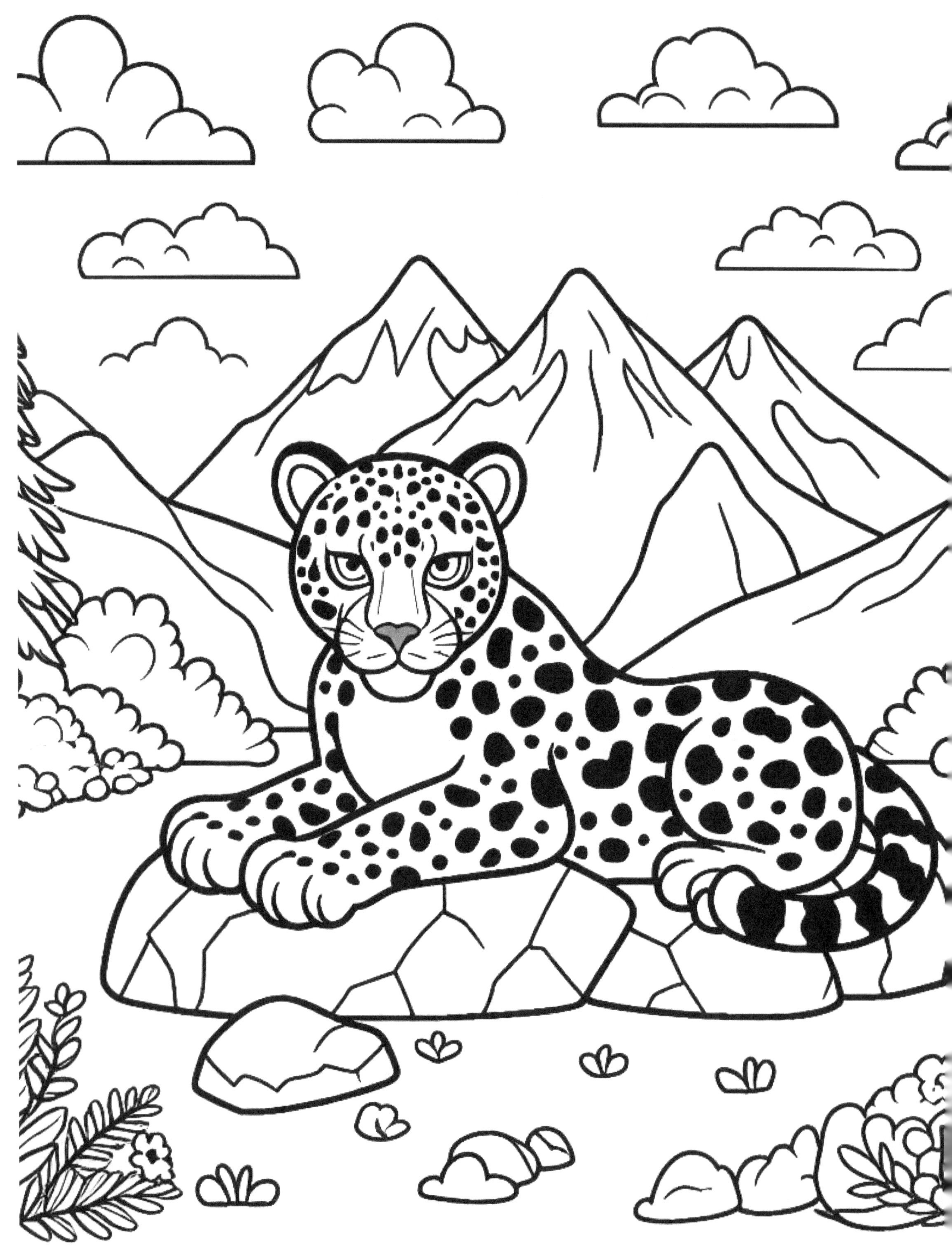

THE MOUNTAIN JAGUAR

The mountain jaguar, also known as the Andean jaguar or the Andean mountain jaguar, is a subspecies of the jaguar (Panthera onca) that inhabits the Andes mountain range in South America. They are the largest big cat in the Americas and are known for their powerful build, distinctive golden-orange coat with black rosettes, and broad head.

Why is the mountain jaguar endangered?

Mountain jaguars face numerous threats to their survival, including habitat loss and fragmentation due to deforestation, human encroachment, and infrastructure development. They are also targeted by poachers for their skins and body parts, and they sometimes come into conflict with livestock owners.

Conservation

Conservation efforts to protect mountain jaguars include the establishment of protected areas, habitat restoration initiatives, anti-poaching patrols, and community-based conservation projects. Research on jaguar ecology and behavior is also important for developing effective conservation strategies.

Overall, the mountain jaguar is a symbol of the rich biodiversity of the Andes and plays a vital role in maintaining the health and balance of its montane ecosystems. Protecting this iconic species and its habitat is essential for ensuring its survival and preserving the natural heritage of South America's highlands.

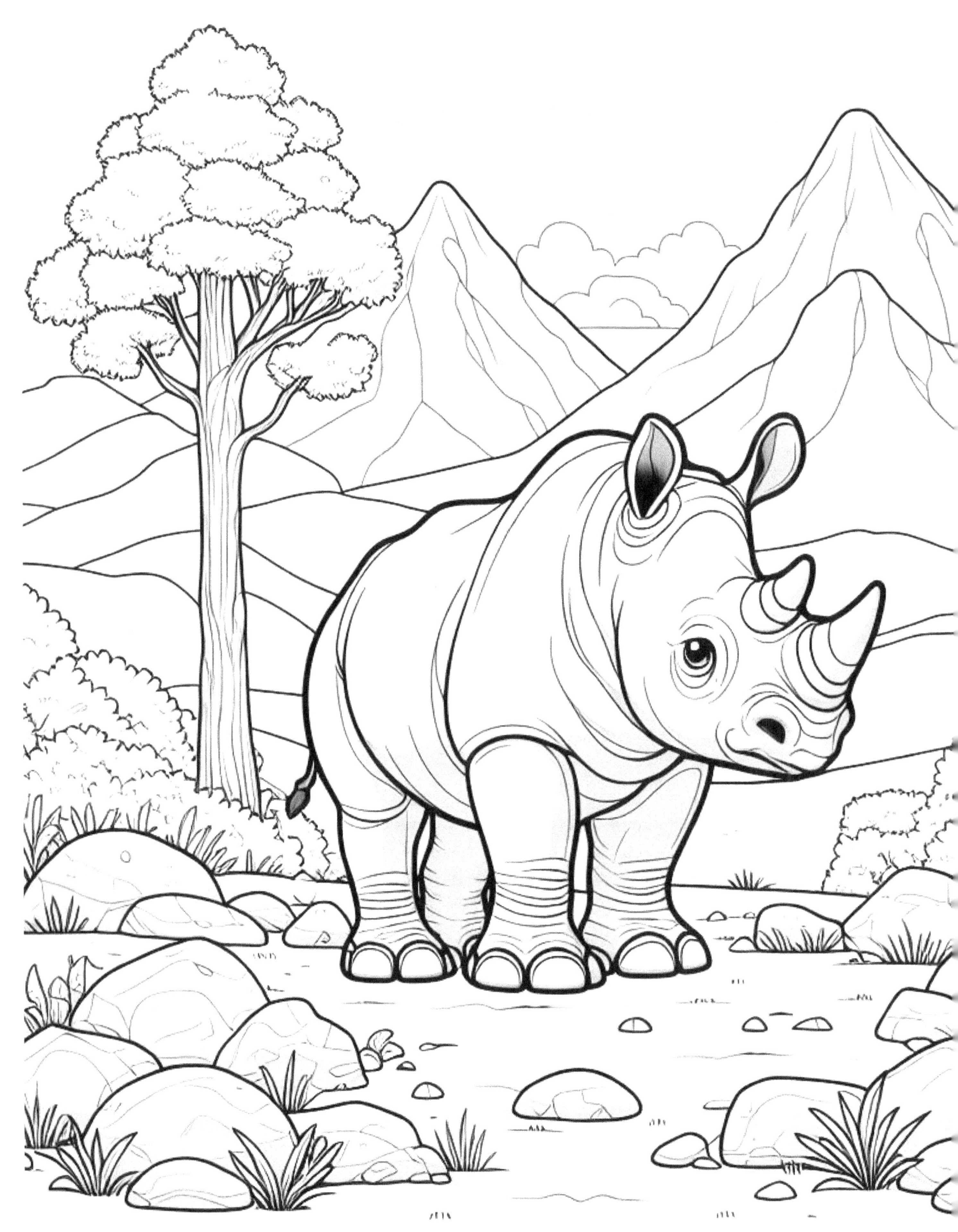

THE BLACK RHINOCEROS

The black rhinoceros is one of the two species of rhinoceros native to Africa, along with the white rhinoceros. It is distinguished by its dark gray to black color, which gives it its name, as well as its prehensile upper lip, adapted for stripping leaves and branches from trees.

Why is the black rhinoceros endangered?

The black rhinoceros is one of the species most affected by poaching. Its horn is highly valued on the black market for its alleged medicinal properties and is considered a status symbol in some cultures. As a result, black rhinoceros populations have declined drastically in recent decades, and the species is classified as "Critically Endangered" by the International Union for Conservation of Nature (IUCN).

Conservation

Various conservation measures are being implemented to protect the black rhinoceros, including anti-poaching patrols, reintroduction programs in protected areas, efforts to reduce the demand for rhinoceros horns, and public awareness campaigns. Despite these efforts, poaching remains a significant threat to the species' survival.

In summary, the black rhinoceros is an iconic species of Africa facing serious threats due to poaching and habitat loss. Protecting this iconic species is crucial for maintaining the biodiversity of African ecosystems and preserving it for future generations.

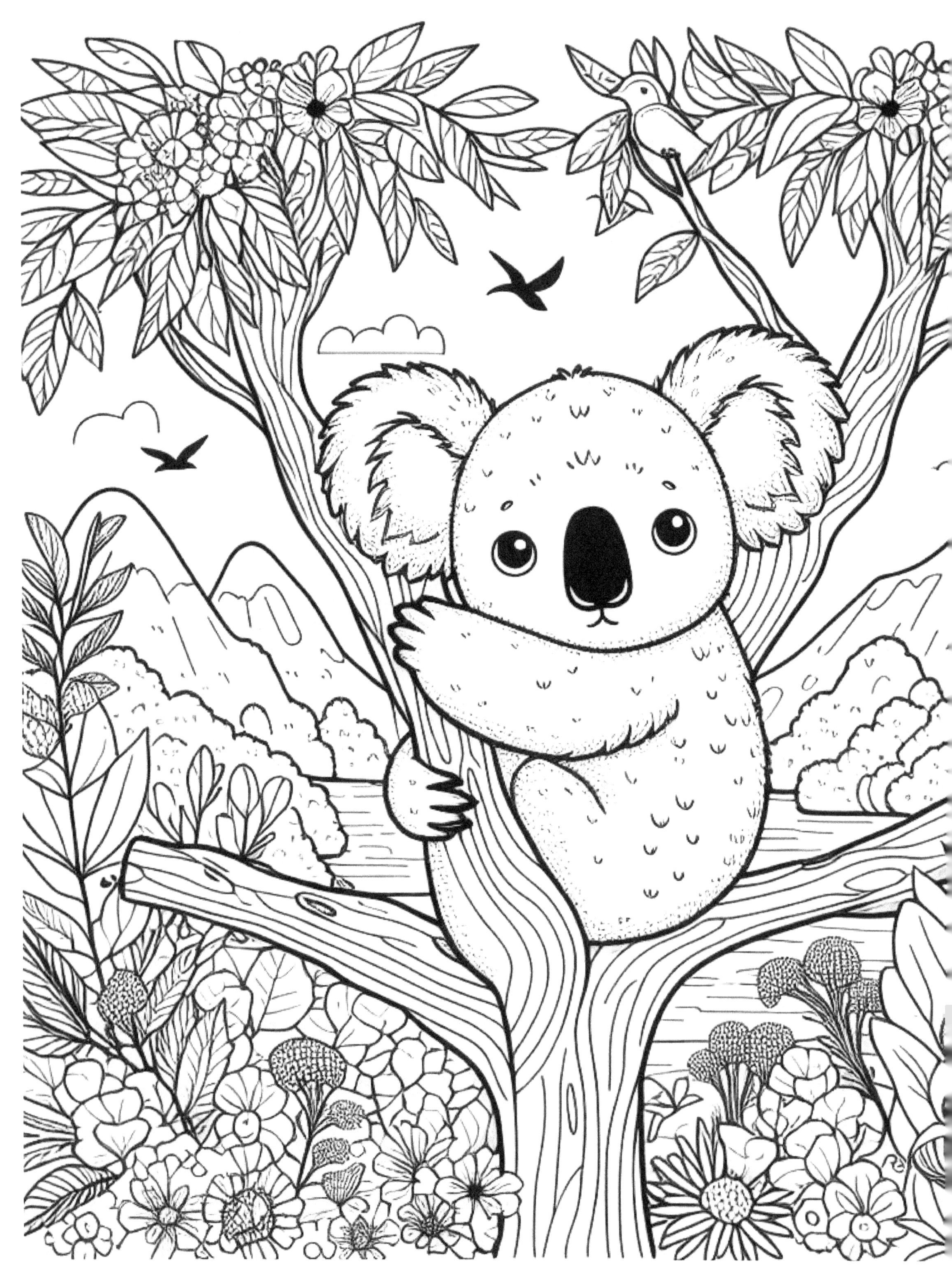

THE KOALA

The koala is an arboreal marsupial native to Australia. These adorable animals are known for their furry appearance, large round nose, and big round eyes.

Why is the koala endangered?

Although koalas are an iconic symbol of Australia, they face numerous threats, including habitat loss and fragmentation, climate change, diseases, wildfires, and predation by animals like dogs and foxes. As a result, some koala populations have declined significantly in recent decades.

Conservation Efforts

Various conservation measures are being implemented to protect koalas, including the creation of wildlife corridors, habitat rehabilitation, conflict mitigation with humans, and disease research. However, ongoing and coordinated efforts are needed to ensure the long-term survival of this iconic Australian species.

In summary, the koala is a beloved symbol of Australian wildlife facing serious threats due to habitat loss and other factors. Protecting koalas and their eucalyptus forests is essential for conserving Australia's biodiversity and ensuring the survival of this unique species in the world.

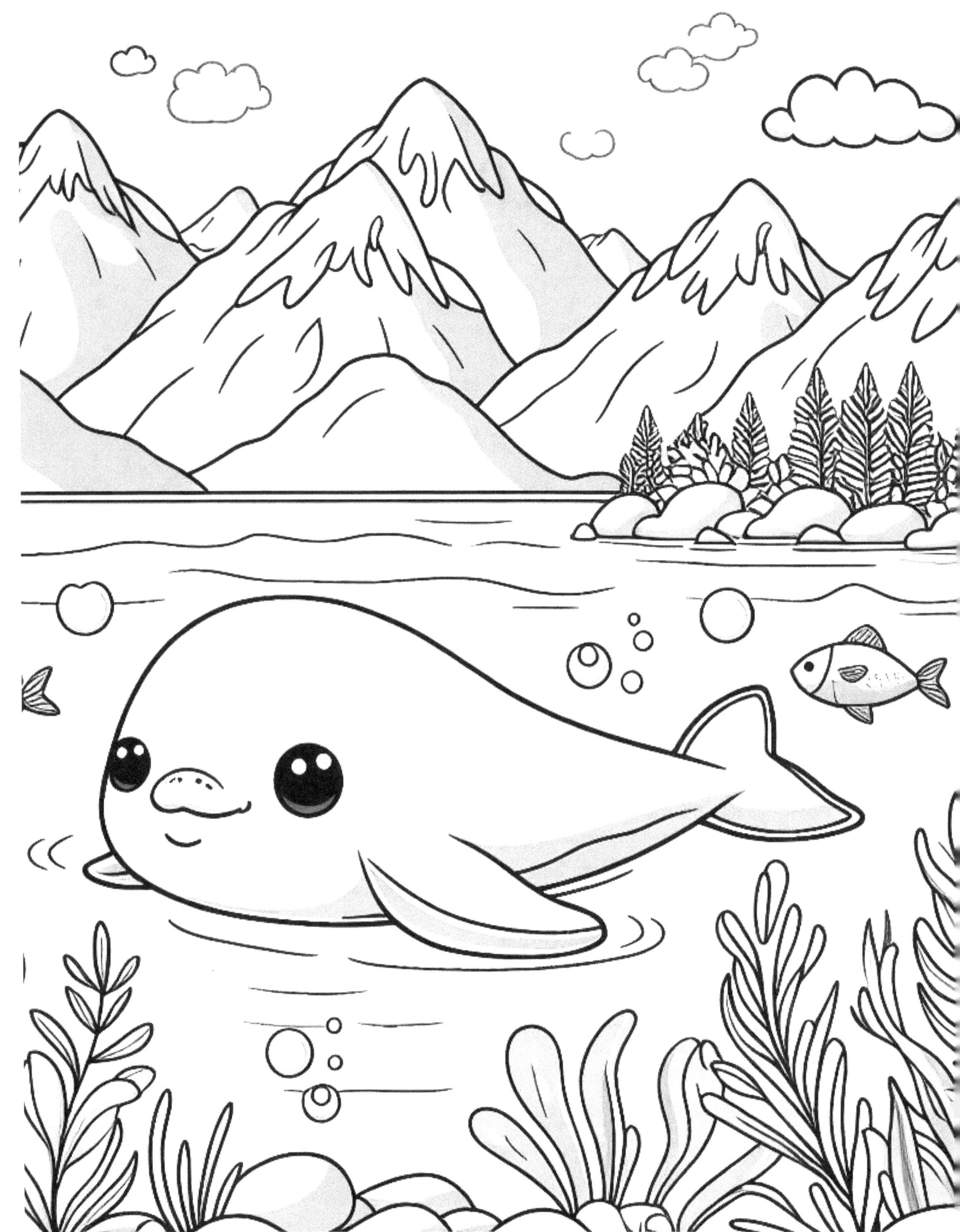

THE VAQUITA PORPOISE

The vaquita (Phocoena sinus) is a species of porpoise endemic to the Gulf of California, Mexico. It is the smallest cetacean in the world and is critically endangered, being one of the most threatened marine species. Here are some highlights about the vaquita:

Why is the vaquita porpoise endangered?

The main threat to the vaquita is illegal fishing for totoaba, a type of fish whose swim bladders are highly valued in the Asian black market. Vaquitas become entangled in gillnets intended to catch totoabas, leading to a rapid decline in their population. Other threats include pollution, climate change, and vessel collisions.

Conservation Status

The vaquita is critically endangered, with fewer than 10 individuals estimated to remain in the wild, making it the most endangered mammal species in the world. Conservation efforts include the prohibition of gillnet fishing in their habitat, surveillance and enforcement programs, as well as efforts to combat the illegal totoaba trade.

Conservation Hope

Despite the challenges, efforts persist to save the vaquita from extinction. This includes the implementation of detection and monitoring technologies, education and awareness about the importance of conservation, and international cooperation to address the illegal totoaba trafficking.

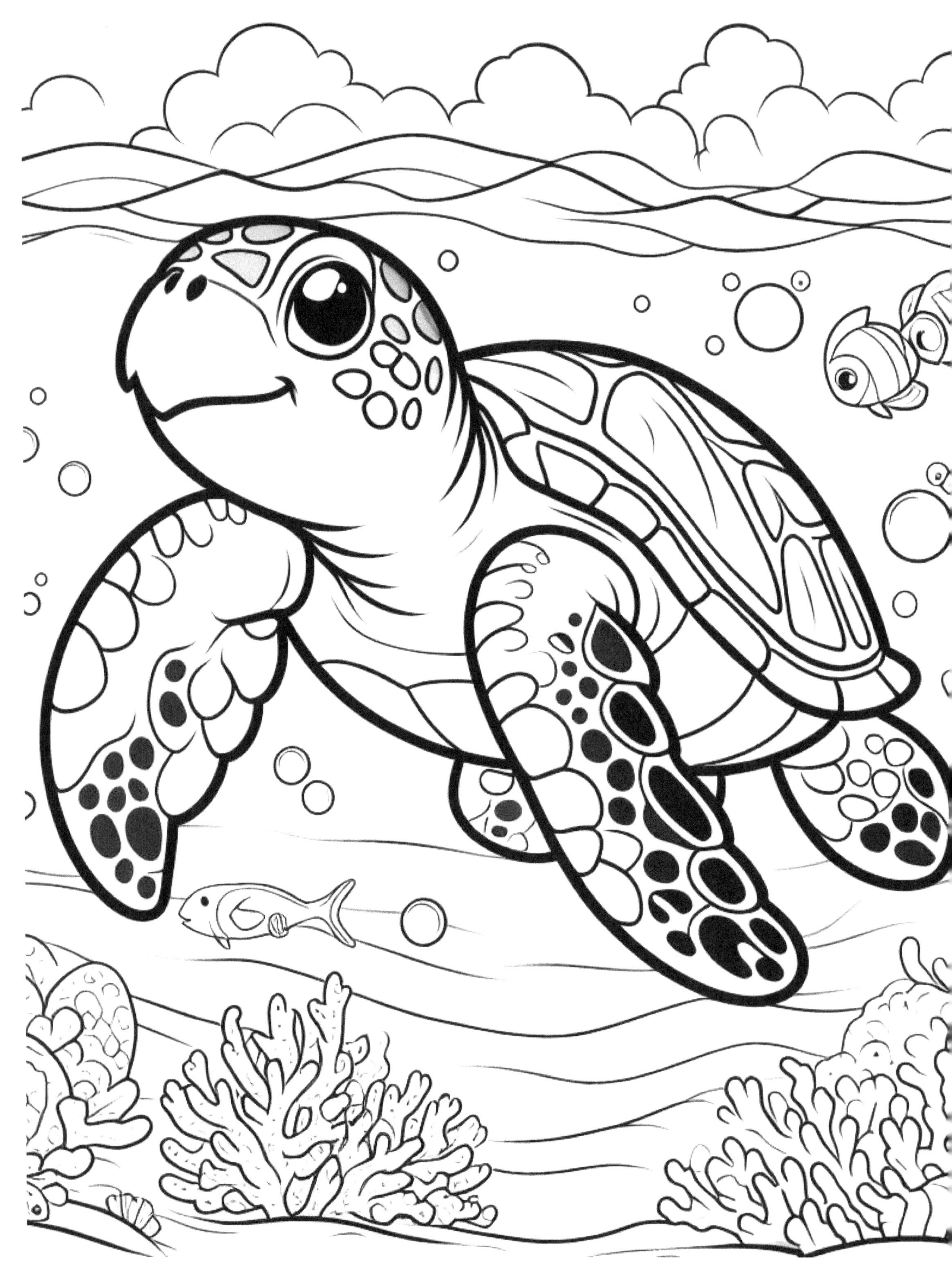

THE LEATHERBACK SEA TURTLE

The leatherback sea turtle is the largest sea turtle species and one of the most unique in the world.

Why is the leatherback sea turtle endangered?

Leatherback turtles face numerous threats, including habitat loss and degradation, marine pollution, incidental capture in fishing gear, climate change, and poaching of eggs and meat. As a result, the leatherback turtle is classified as "Vulnerable" on the IUCN Red List. Conservation efforts are underway worldwide to protect this species, including the establishment of marine protected areas, regulation of bycatch, and public education on the importance of conservation.

In summary, the leatherback sea turtle is a fascinating and emblematic species facing a range of challenges in its marine habitat. Protecting these majestic creatures is essential for maintaining the health of ocean ecosystems and preserving their legacy for future generations.

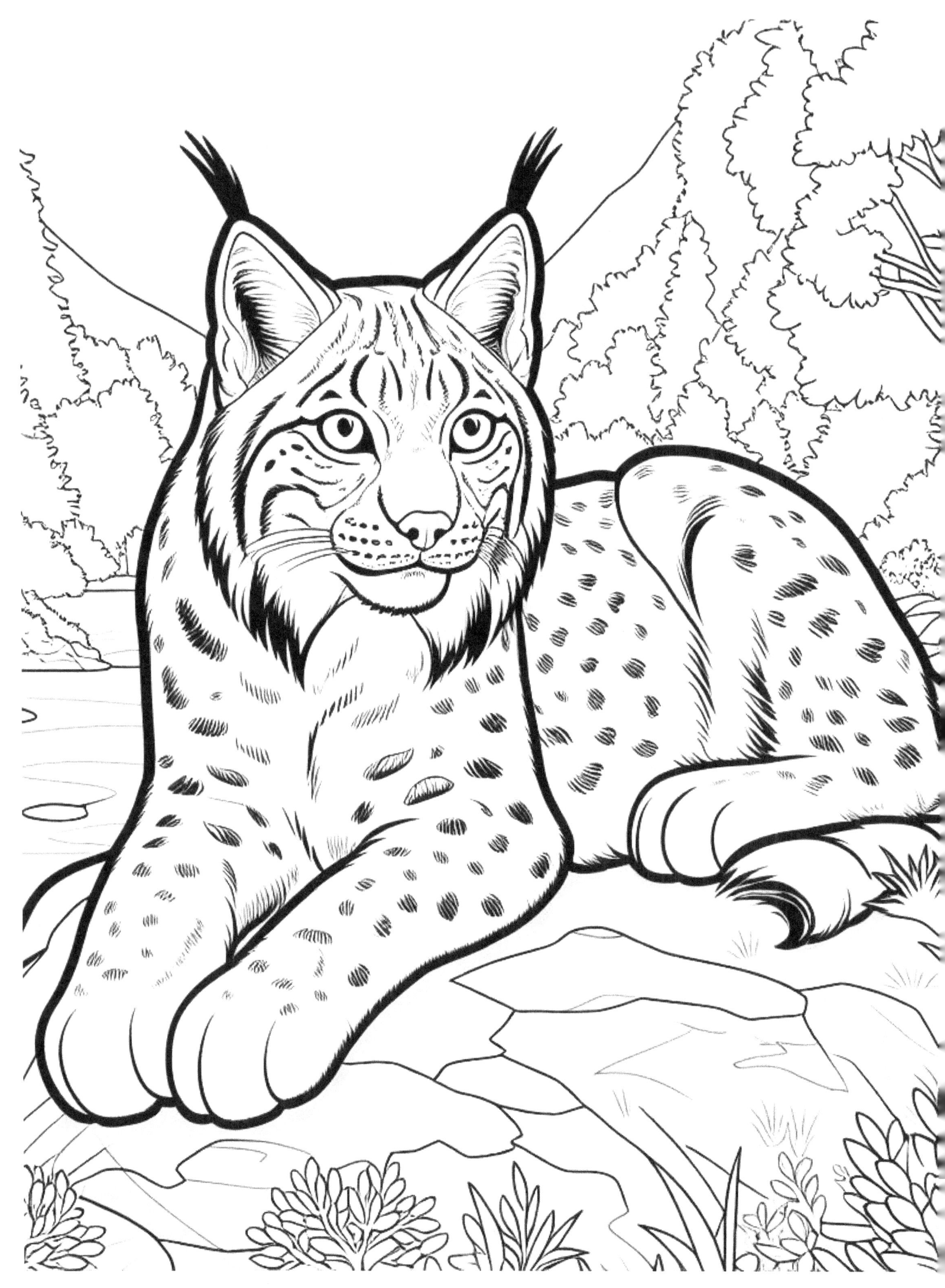

THE IBERIAN LYNX

The Iberian lynx is a species of feline endemic to the Iberian Peninsula, which includes Spain and Portugal. Here are some highlights about the Iberian lynx:

Why is the Iberian lynx endangered?

The Iberian lynx has faced numerous threats over the years, including habitat loss and fragmentation, poaching, diseases, roadkill, and the scarcity of natural prey due to declining rabbit populations. In response to this critical situation, various conservation programs have been implemented, including captive breeding, reintroduction into historical distribution areas, and habitat improvement.

Conservation

Despite challenges, conservation efforts have been successful in stabilizing and increasing Iberian lynx populations in certain areas. This has been possible thanks to collaboration between governmental organizations, NGOs, scientists, and the involvement of local communities.

In summary, the Iberian lynx is an emblematic feline of the Iberian Peninsula that has faced serious threats in the past but has proven resilient thanks to conservation efforts. Protecting this unique species is crucial for preserving the biodiversity of Mediterranean ecosystems and ensuring its long-term survival.

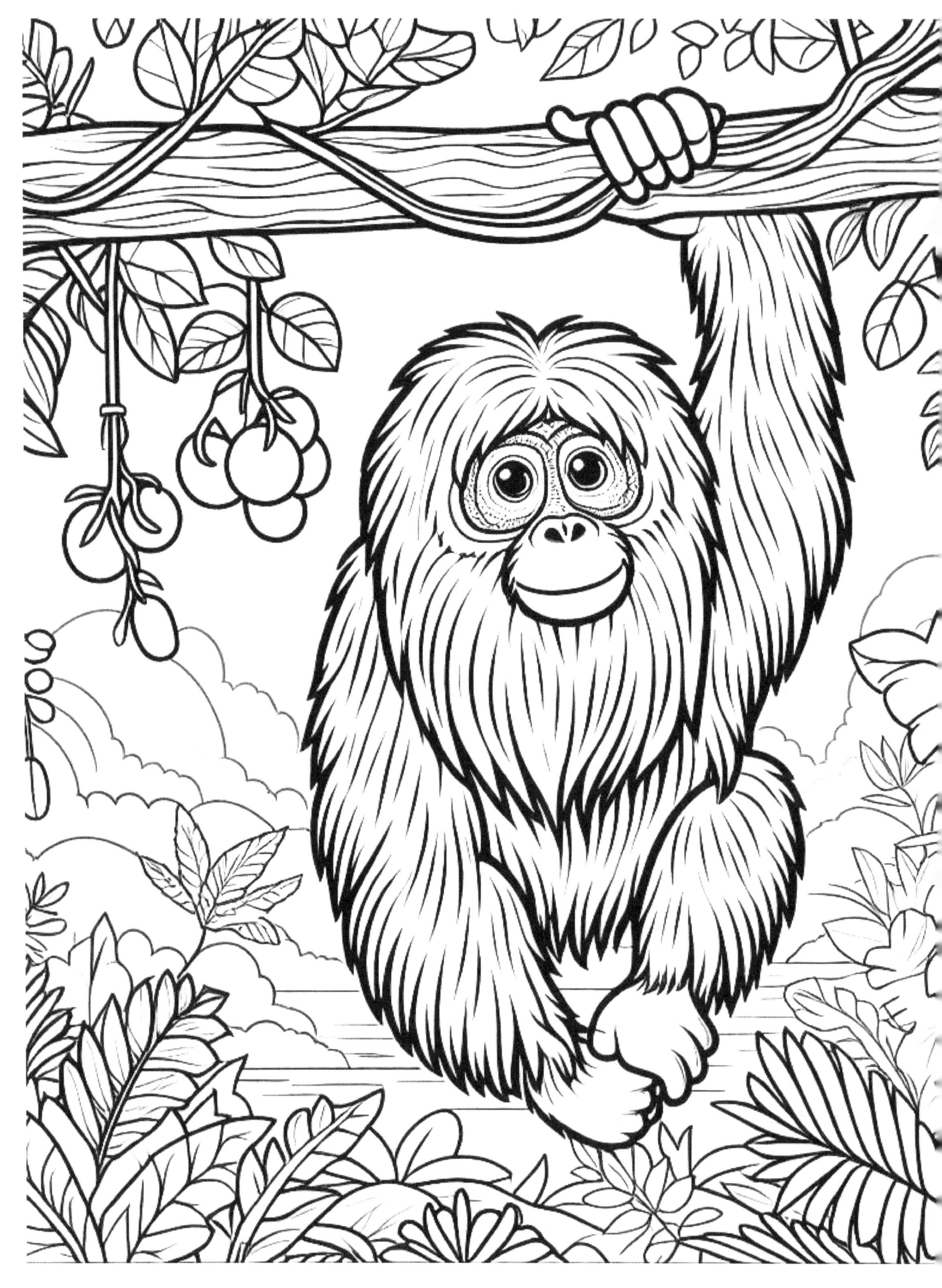

SUMATRAN ORANGUTAN

The Sumatran orangutan is one of the three species of orangutans, which are the only great apes found outside of Africa.

Why is the Sumatran orangutan endangered?

Sumatran orangutans are critically endangered due to habitat loss and fragmentation caused by deforestation, conversion of forests for agriculture (such as palm oil plantations), illegal logging, and human-wildlife conflict. They are also threatened by poaching and the illegal pet trade. Conservation efforts include the establishment of protected areas, community-based conservation projects, reforestation efforts, and campaigns to promote sustainable palm oil production and consumption.

Conservation

According to the IUCN Red List of Threatened Species, Sumatran orangutans are classified as critically endangered. It is estimated that there are fewer than 14,000 individuals remaining in the wild, and their population is declining. Urgent action is needed to protect their remaining habitat and ensure their survival.

In summary, the Sumatran orangutan is a critically endangered species facing severe threats to its survival. Conservation efforts are crucial to protect their habitat and address the various human-induced pressures threatening their existence.

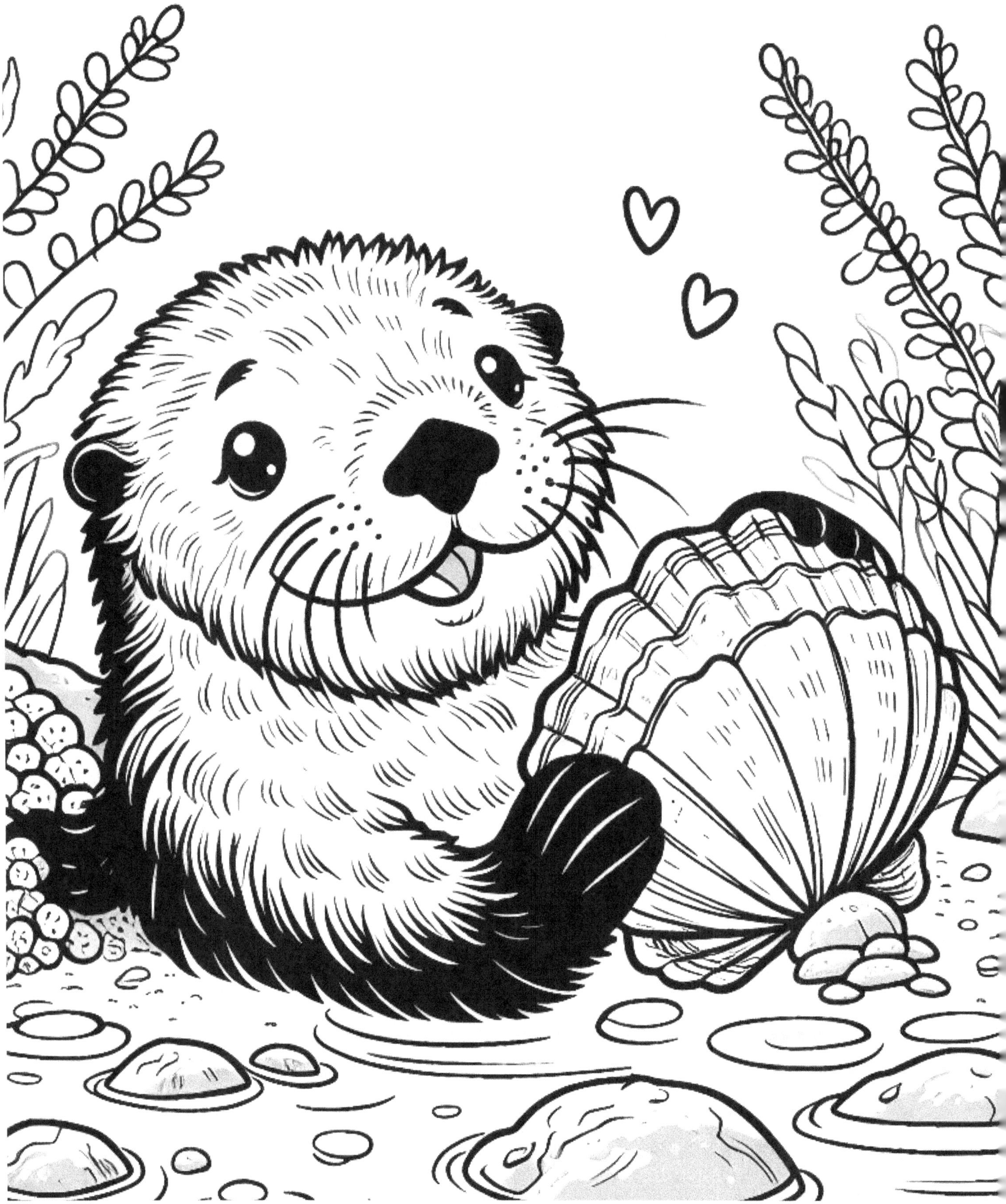

THE SEA OTTER

The sea otter, also known as marine otter or sea wolf, is a highly specialized marine mammal that inhabits the cold waters of the North Pacific Ocean, from northern Japan and Kamchatka to the central coast of California in the United States.

Why is the sea otter endangered?

In the early 20th century, sea otter populations were severely depleted due to overhunting for their valuable fur. However, thanks to conservation and protection efforts, sea otter populations have recovered in many areas of their range.

Although sea otters have experienced a recovery in some areas, they still face threats, including loss and degradation of coastal habitat, marine pollution, incidental fishing, and climate change. Continued protection of their habitat and sustainable management of human activities are crucial to ensuring the long-term survival of this species.

In summary, the sea otter is a fascinating and emblematic marine mammal that plays an important role in the coastal ecosystems of the North Pacific Ocean. While they have experienced recovery in some areas, ongoing conservation efforts are essential to ensure their survival and protect their habitat.

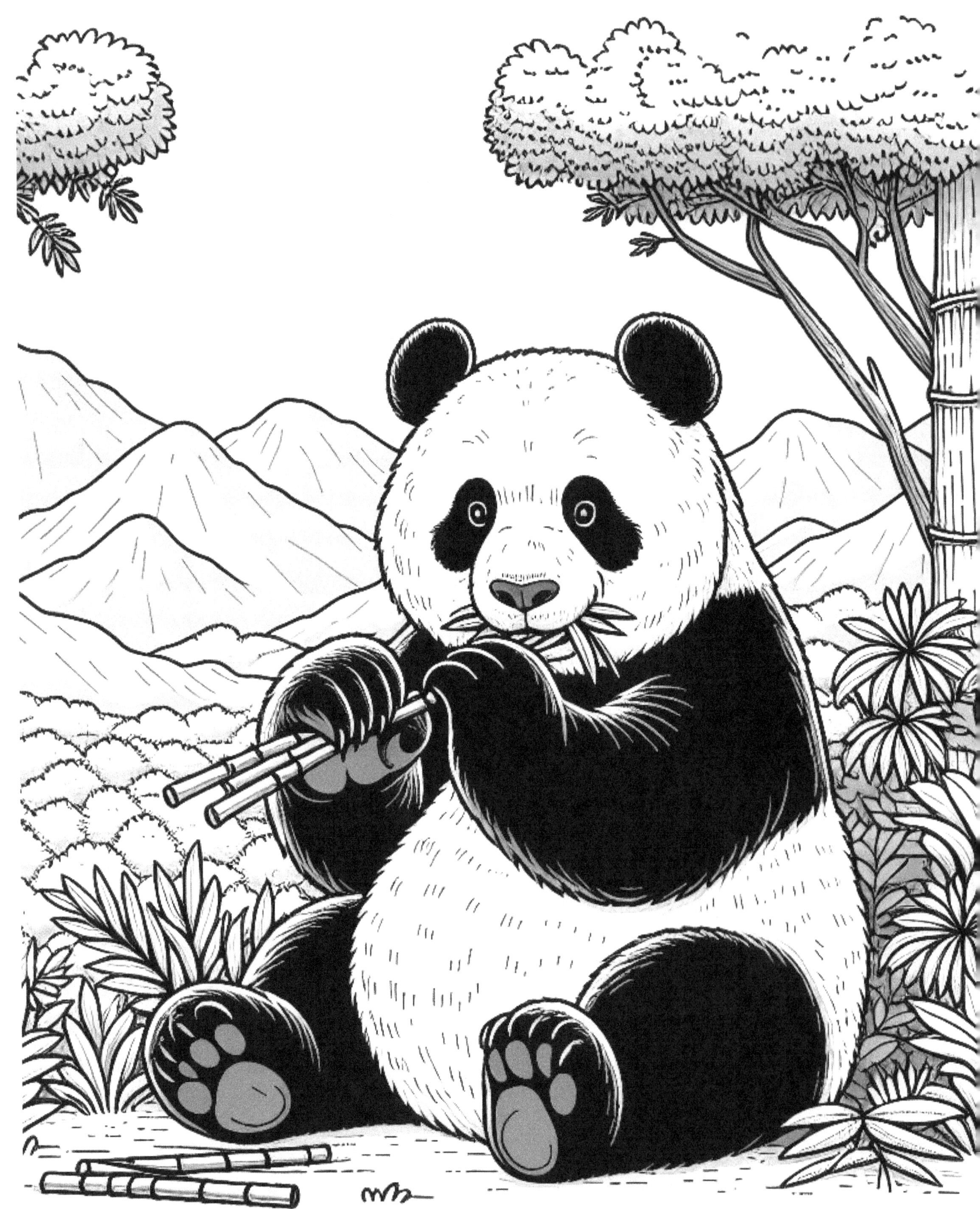

THE GIANT PANDA, OR PANDA BEAR

The giant panda, or panda bear (Ailuropoda melanoleuca), is a beloved and iconic symbol of conservation efforts worldwide.

Why is the giant panda endangered?

Giant pandas are classified as "Vulnerable" on the IUCN Red List of Threatened Species, with habitat loss and fragmentation being the primary threats to their survival. Conservation efforts, including habitat protection, captive breeding programs, and public awareness campaigns, have helped stabilize giant panda populations in recent years.

In summary, the giant panda is an iconic and beloved species that has captured the hearts of people worldwide. While their future remains uncertain due to ongoing threats, concerted conservation efforts offer hope for the long-term survival of this remarkable species.

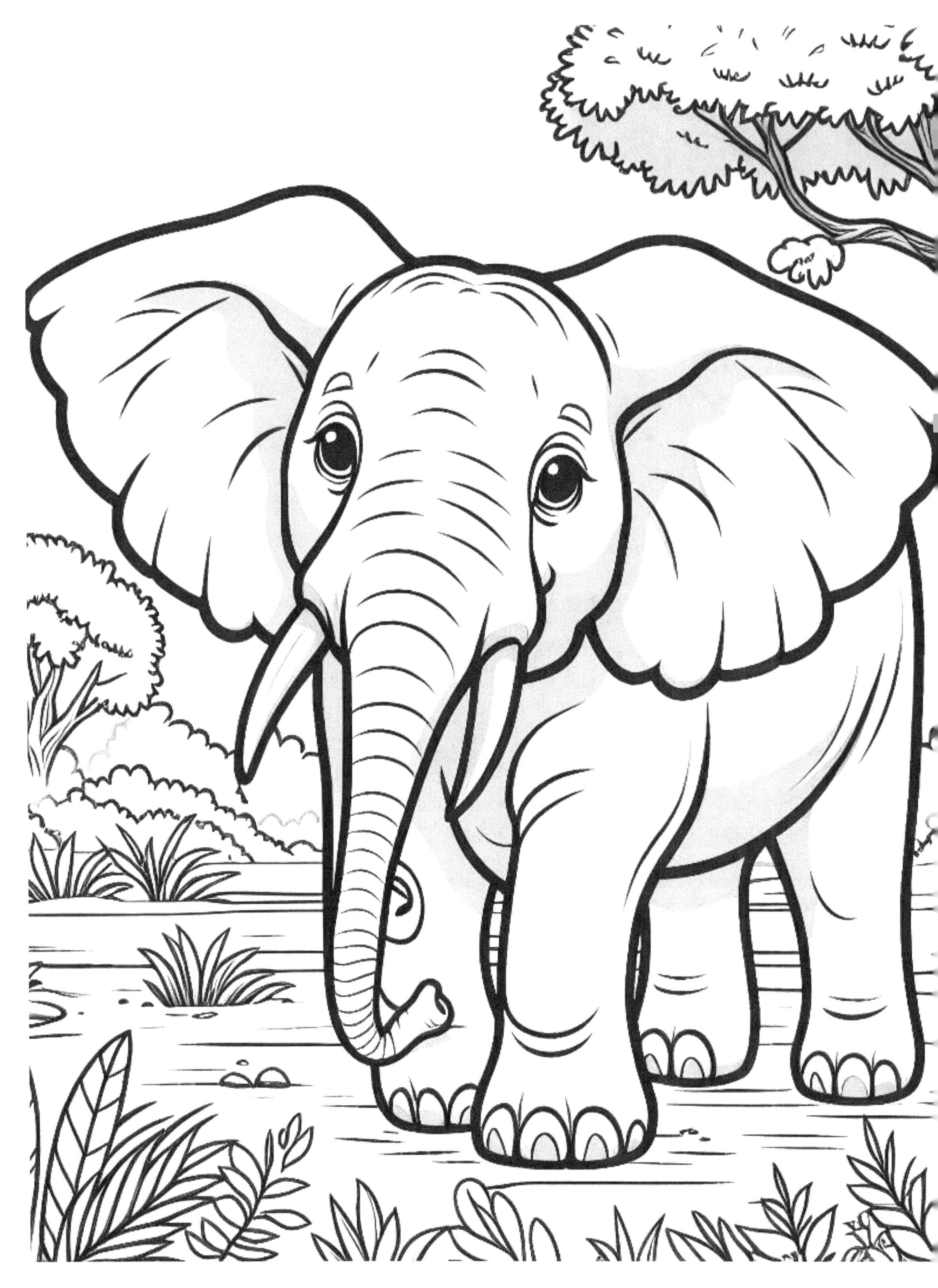

THE AFRICAN ELEPHANT

The African elephant is a majestic and iconic species that inhabits various regions of Africa.

Why is the African elephant endangered?

African elephants face numerous threats, including habitat loss due to human expansion, poaching for their ivory tusks, human-elephant conflicts, and habitat fragmentation. As a result, they have experienced significant population declines in recent decades. Conservation efforts for African elephants include measures to protect their habitat, combat poaching, and promote peaceful coexistence between humans and elephants.

In summary, the African elephant is an iconic and keystone species for African ecosystems and the culture of many communities in Africa. Their conservation is crucial to ensure the health of ecosystems and the long-term survival of this magnificent species.

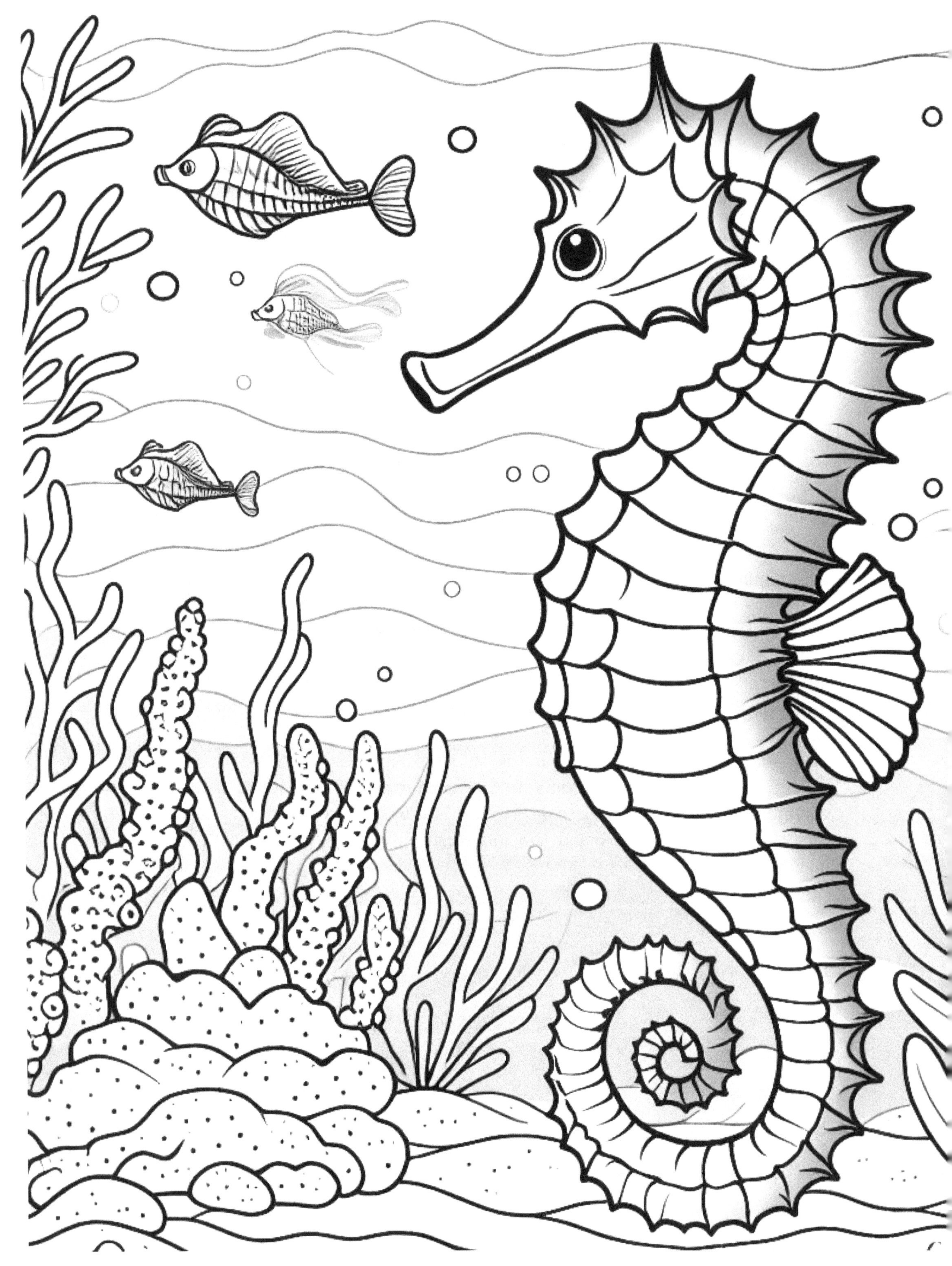

THE SEAHORSE

The seahorse is a unique and fascinating marine creature belonging to the family Syngnathidae, which also includes pipefish and seadragons.

Why is the seahorse endangered?

Seahorses face various threats, including habitat loss, water pollution, accidental capture in fishing gear, and illegal trade for use in traditional medicine and as pets. Many seahorse species are at risk of overexploitation and extinction, leading to the implementation of conservation and regulatory measures in some countries.

Ecological Importance

Despite their small size, seahorses play an important role in marine ecosystems as population control predators and prey for other marine animals. Their presence indicates the health of coastal habitats and marine biodiversity.

In summary, seahorses are unique and fascinating marine creatures with a remarkable lifestyle and adaptations. However, they face numerous threats in their natural habitat and require protection and conservation to ensure their long-term survival.

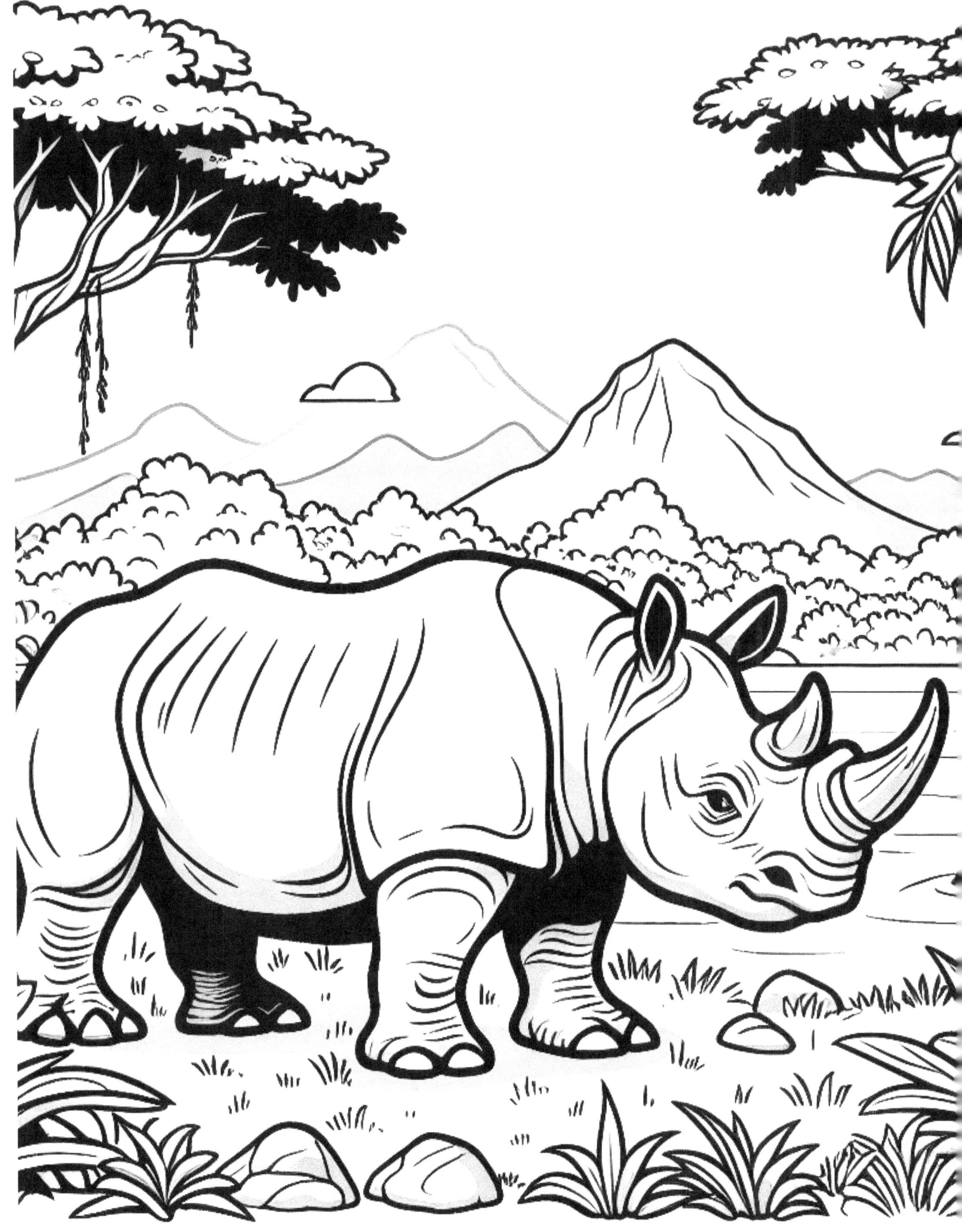

THE JAVAN RHINOCEROS

The Javan rhinoceros is a species of rhinoceros that inhabits forested regions of Indonesia and Vietnam.

Why is the Javan rhinoceros endangered?

The Javan rhinoceros faces numerous threats, including habitat loss due to deforestation, poaching for their horns, and habitat fragmentation due to agricultural expansion and human development. As a result, there are estimated to be fewer than 70 individuals remaining in the wild, making it one of the most critically endangered mammal species in the world.

Conservation

Intensive conservation efforts are underway to protect the Javan rhinoceros and increase its population. These include protection patrols to combat poaching, habitat management and restoration, and captive breeding programs with the goal of reintroducing individuals into the wild.

In summary, the Javan rhinoceros is a critically endangered species facing severe threats to its survival. Effective conservation of its habitat and protection against poaching are crucial to ensuring the long-term survival of this unique and valuable species.

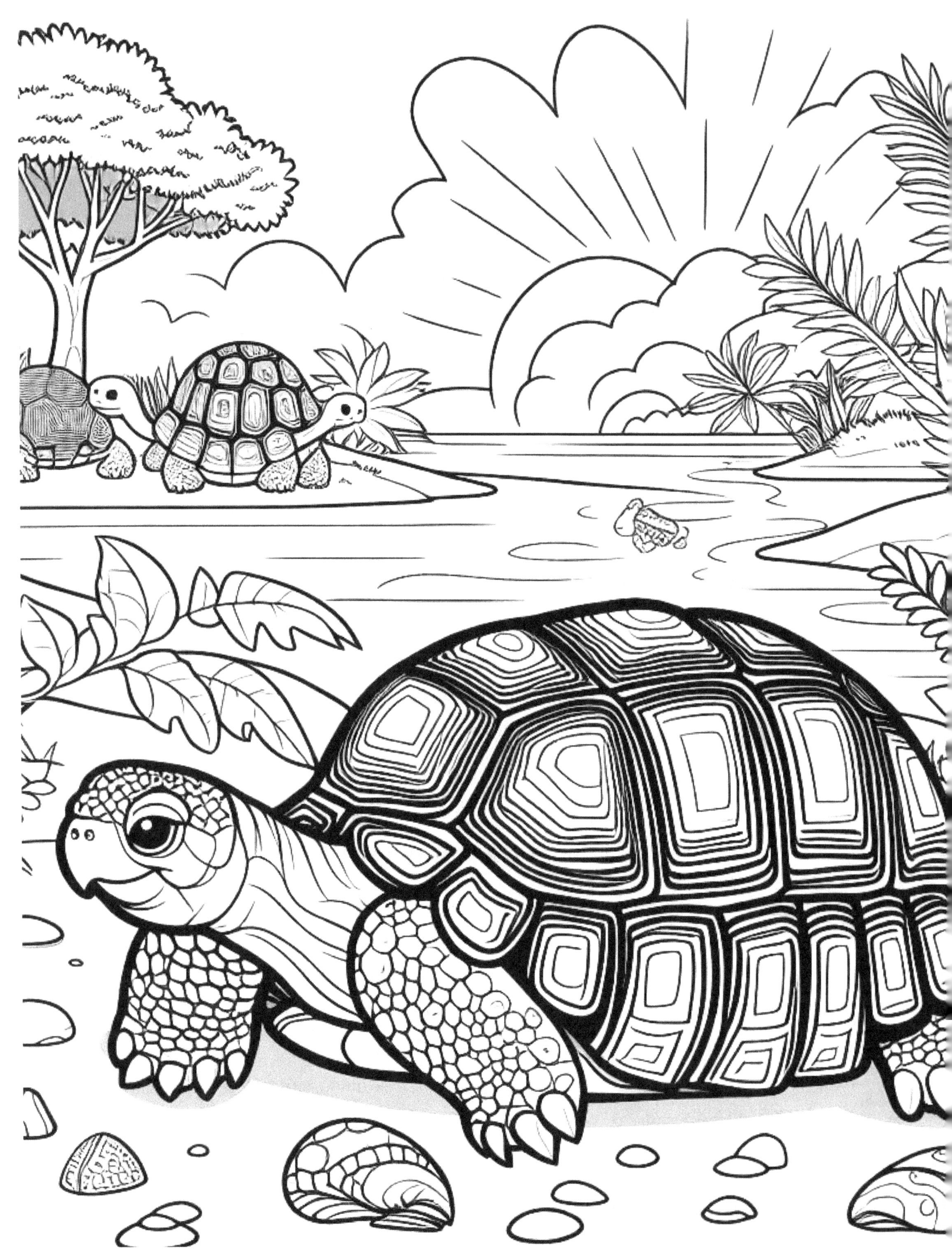

THE AFRICAN SPURRED TORTOISE

The African spurred tortoise, also known as the sulcata tortoise (Geochelone sulcata), is a species of terrestrial tortoise native to sub-Saharan Africa.

Why is the African spurred tortoise endangered?

Despite their popularity as pets, African spurred tortoises face threats in the wild due to habitat loss, hunting for the pet trade, and environmental degradation. Conservation efforts for this species include measures to protect their natural habitat and regulate the international trade of wild-caught specimens.

In summary, the African spurred tortoise is a fascinating and resilient species found across various countries in sub-Saharan Africa. While they are popular as pets, it is important to address the threats they face in the wild to ensure their long-term survival.

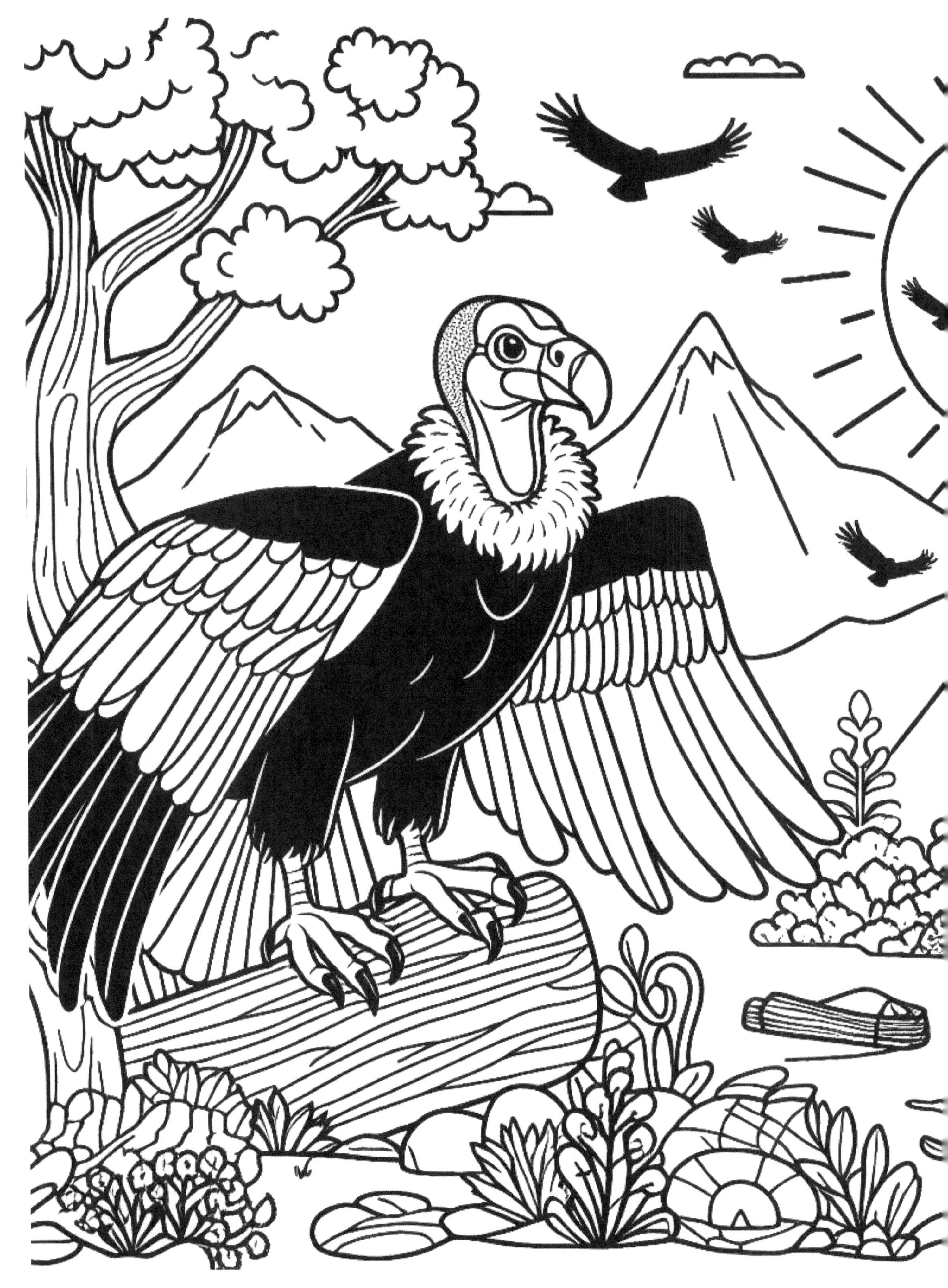

THE CALIFORNIA CONDOR

The California condor (Gymnogyps californianus) is a species of large and majestic scavenging bird that inhabits mountainous and coastal regions of western North America.

Conservation and Recovery

By the late 20th century, the California condor was on the brink of extinction due to habitat loss, poaching, and lead poisoning. However, thanks to intensive conservation efforts, including captive breeding programs and the reintroduction of individuals into the wild, the California condor population has gradually increased in recent decades.

Current Threats

Although there have been strides in the species' recovery, the California condor still faces significant threats, including lead exposure from consuming contaminated carrion, habitat loss due to human development, and collisions with power lines and wind turbines.

In summary, the California condor is an emblematic species that has been rescued from the brink of extinction thanks to conservation efforts. However, it still faces challenges, and ongoing habitat protection and threat reduction are crucial to ensuring its long-term survival.

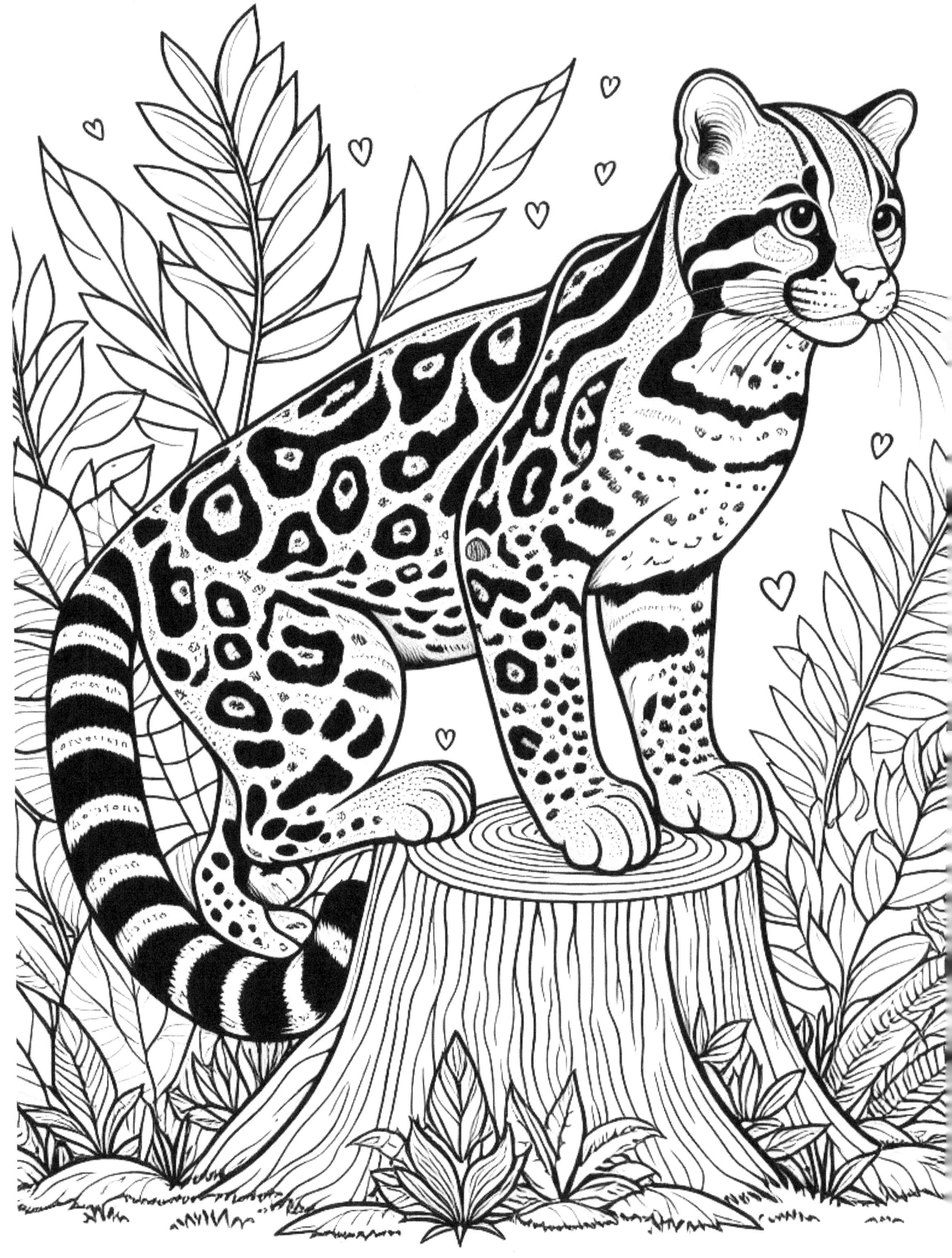

THE OCELOT

The ocelot is a medium-sized wild cat that inhabits Latin America and parts of the southern United States.

Why is the ocelot endangered?

Ocelots face numerous threats, including habitat loss and fragmentation due to deforestation and agricultural expansion, poaching for their fur, and direct persecution due to conflicts with humans. As a result, some ocelot populations are declining and are listed as endangered species in certain areas.

Conservation

Efforts to protect ocelots include the creation of protected areas, the implementation of biological corridors to facilitate movement between fragmented habitats, and public education about the importance of wildlife conservation.

In summary, the ocelot is a fascinating and adaptable wild cat that plays a significant role in the ecosystems where it inhabits. However, it faces numerous threats due to human activity and requires ongoing conservation efforts to ensure its long-term survival.

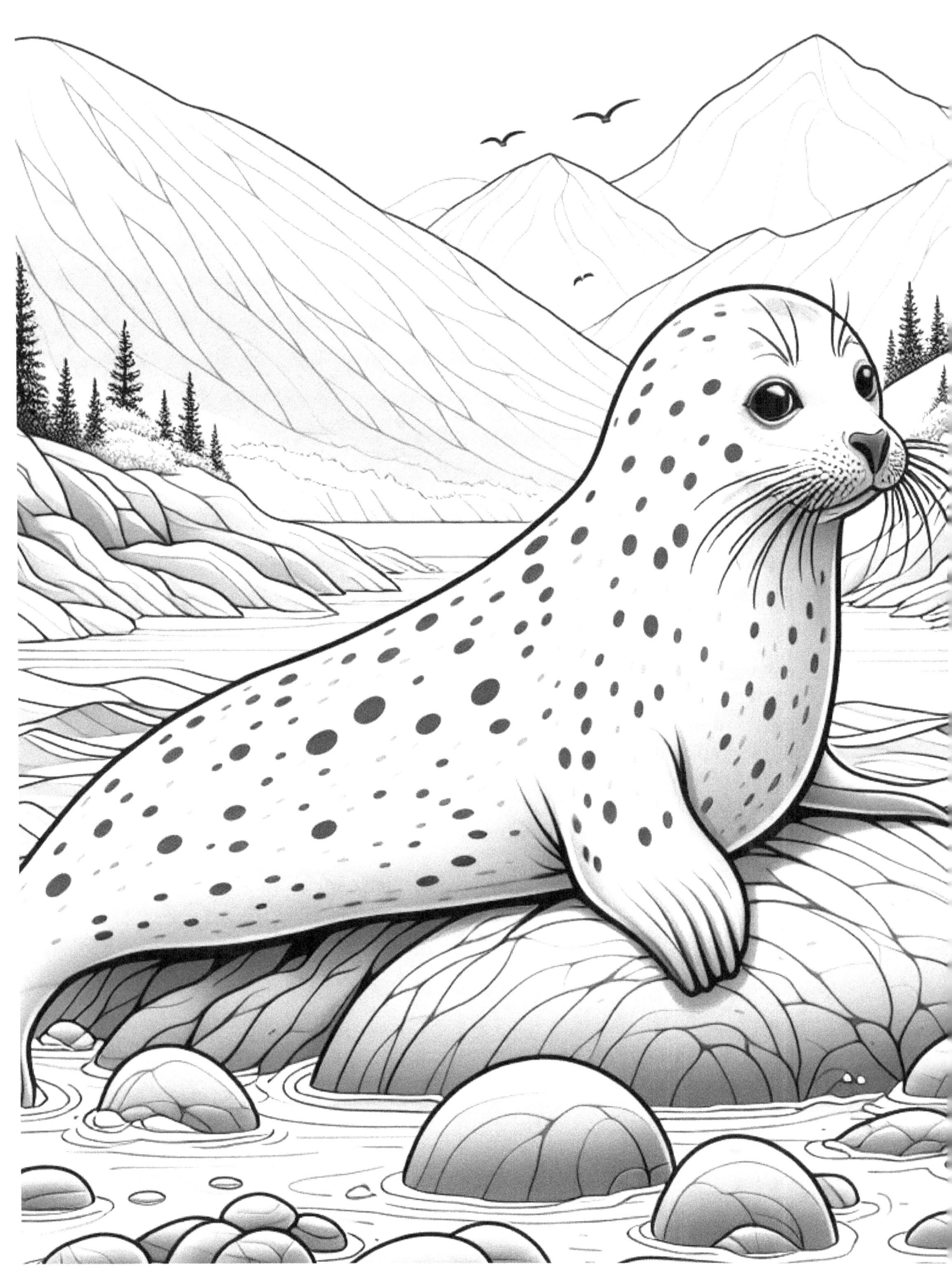

THE RINGED SEAL

The ringed seal, also known as the Pusa hispida, is a species of seal that inhabits the Arctic and subarctic regions, including the Arctic Ocean, the Beaufort Sea, the Chukchi Sea, and the Bering Sea.

Why is the ringed seal endangered?

Ringed seals face several threats, including habitat loss due to climate change and the decline in sea ice extent. They are also subject to commercial hunting in some areas and may become accidentally trapped in fishing nets.

Ecological Importance

These seals play an important role in Arctic ecosystems as top predators, regulating the populations of their prey and contributing to the overall health of the marine ecosystem.

In summary, the ringed seal is an iconic species of the Arctic and subarctic regions that faces challenges due to climate change and human activity. Their conservation is crucial for maintaining biodiversity and the health of Arctic ecosystems.

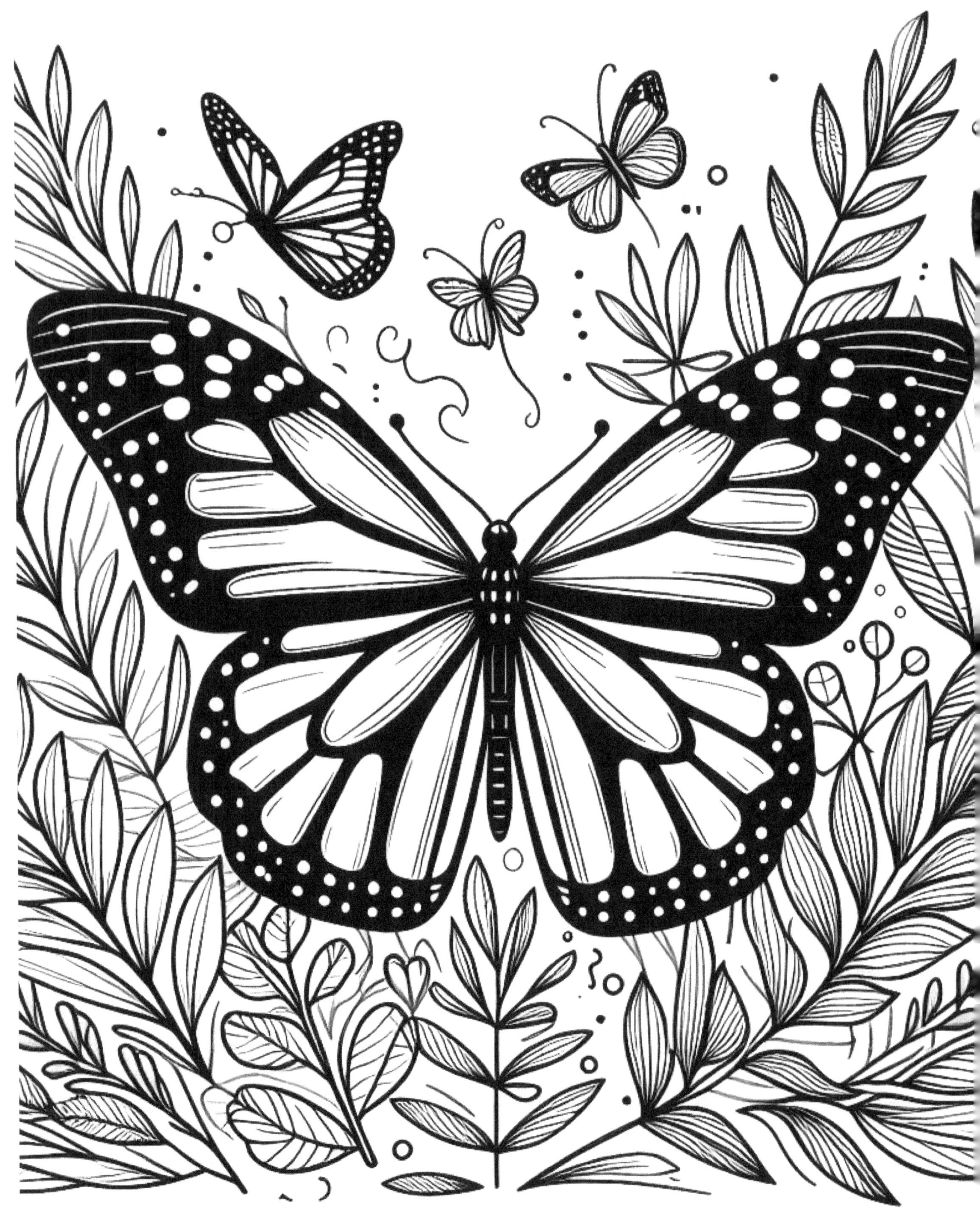

THE MONARCH BUTTERFLY

The monarch butterfly is a species of butterfly known for its astonishing annual migration and distinctive orange and black color pattern.

Why is the monarch butterfly endangered?

The monarch butterfly faces numerous threats, including habitat loss due to urbanization and intensive agriculture, the use of pesticides and herbicides that affect milkweed plants, and climate change that alters migration patterns and winter climate in Mexico.

Despite the challenges, there is hope for the conservation of the monarch butterfly. Conservation efforts are underway along its entire migration route, including the protection of key habitats, the planting of milkweed plants, and public education about the importance of preserving this unique species and its habitats.

In summary, the monarch butterfly is an iconic and fascinating butterfly that undertakes an extraordinary migration every year. Its conservation is crucial for maintaining the health of ecosystems and the beauty of nature.

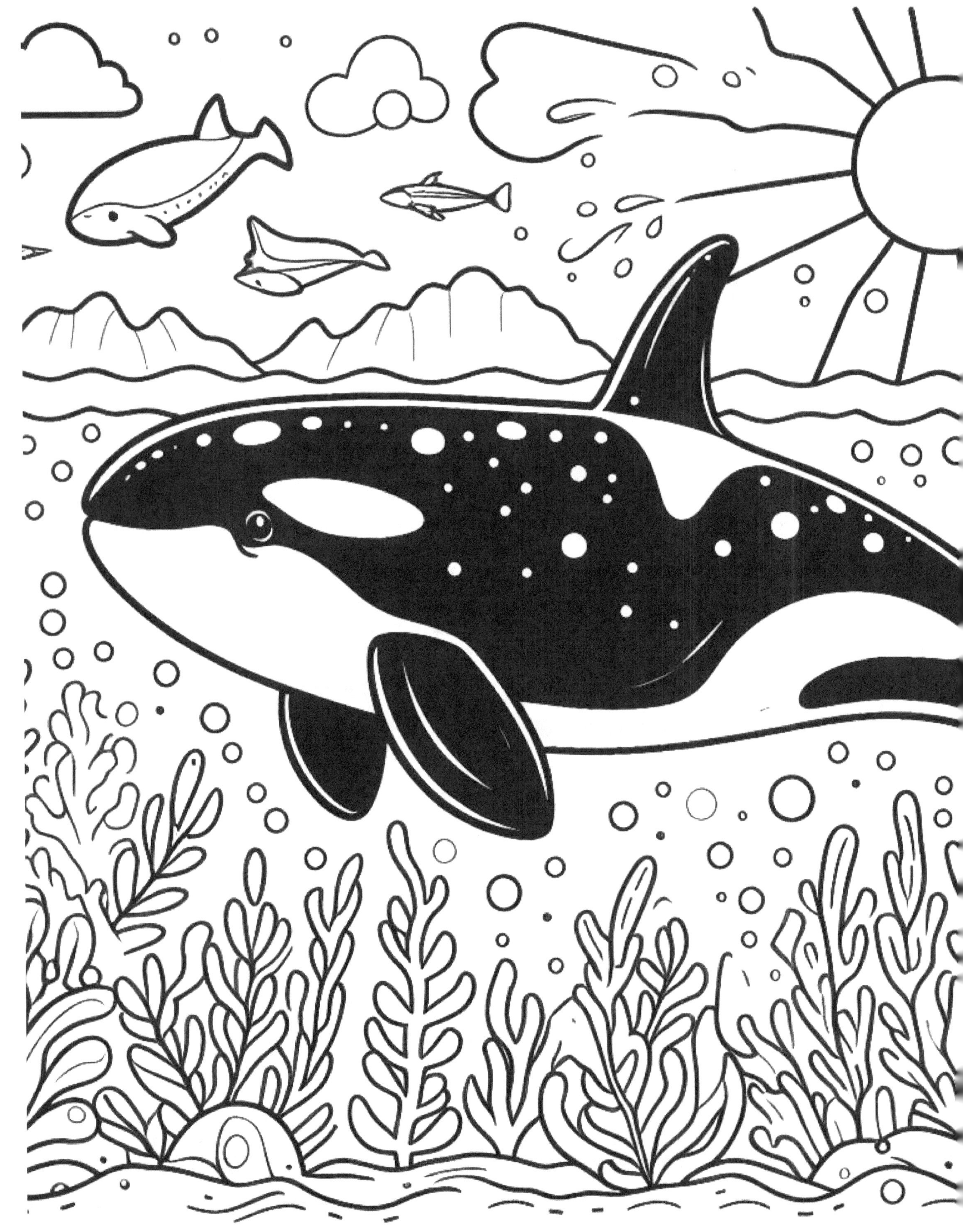

THE KILLER WHALE

The killer whale, also known as the orca (Orcinus orca), is a species of cetacean belonging to the dolphin family (Delphinidae).

Conservation and Threats

Despite being one of the most widely distributed and recognized cetacean species, killer whales face numerous threats, including water pollution, habitat loss, human interference such as underwater noise and vessel collisions, and declining prey populations due to overfishing. Although not classified as endangered species, some killer whale populations are declining and require appropriate conservation and management measures to protect them.

In summary, the killer whale is one of the most iconic and fascinating creatures of the world's oceans, known for its intelligence, cooperative hunting skills, and crucial role in marine ecosystems. Its conservation is essential to maintain the health and biodiversity of the oceans.

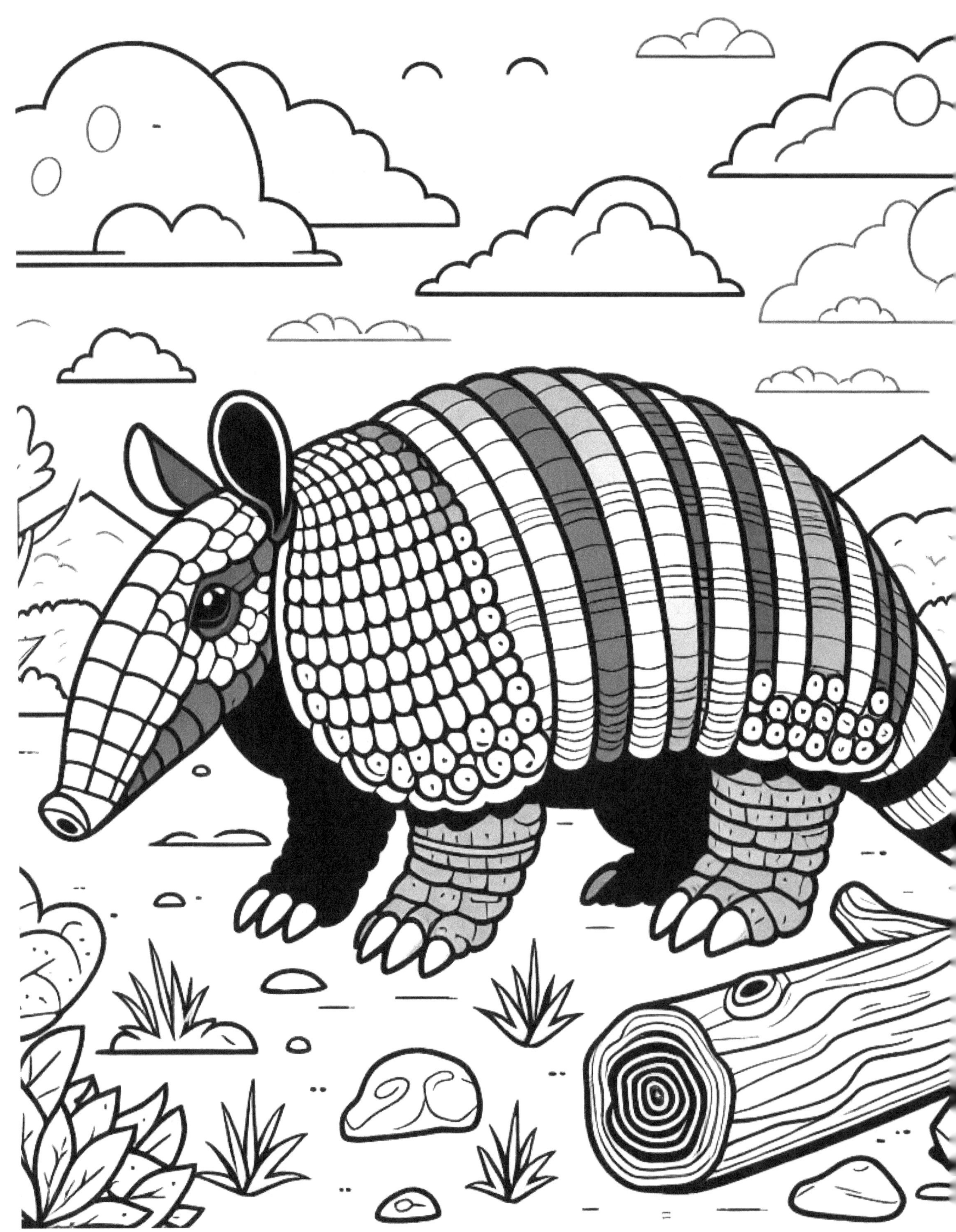

THE GIANT ARMADILLO

The giant armadillo (Priodontes maximus), also known as the giant anteater or great anteater, is a species of mammal belonging to the Dasypodidae family, known for its considerable size and protective armor.

Why is the giant armadillo endangered?

The giant armadillo faces various threats, including habitat loss and fragmentation due to agricultural and urban expansion. It is also hunted for its meat and armor, leading to declines in some populations. Additionally, soil and water pollution also pose risks to its survival.

In summary, the giant armadillo is a fascinating and unique species that plays an important role in the ecosystems where it inhabits. However, it faces significant challenges due to human activity, and conservation of its habitat is crucial to ensure its long-term survival.

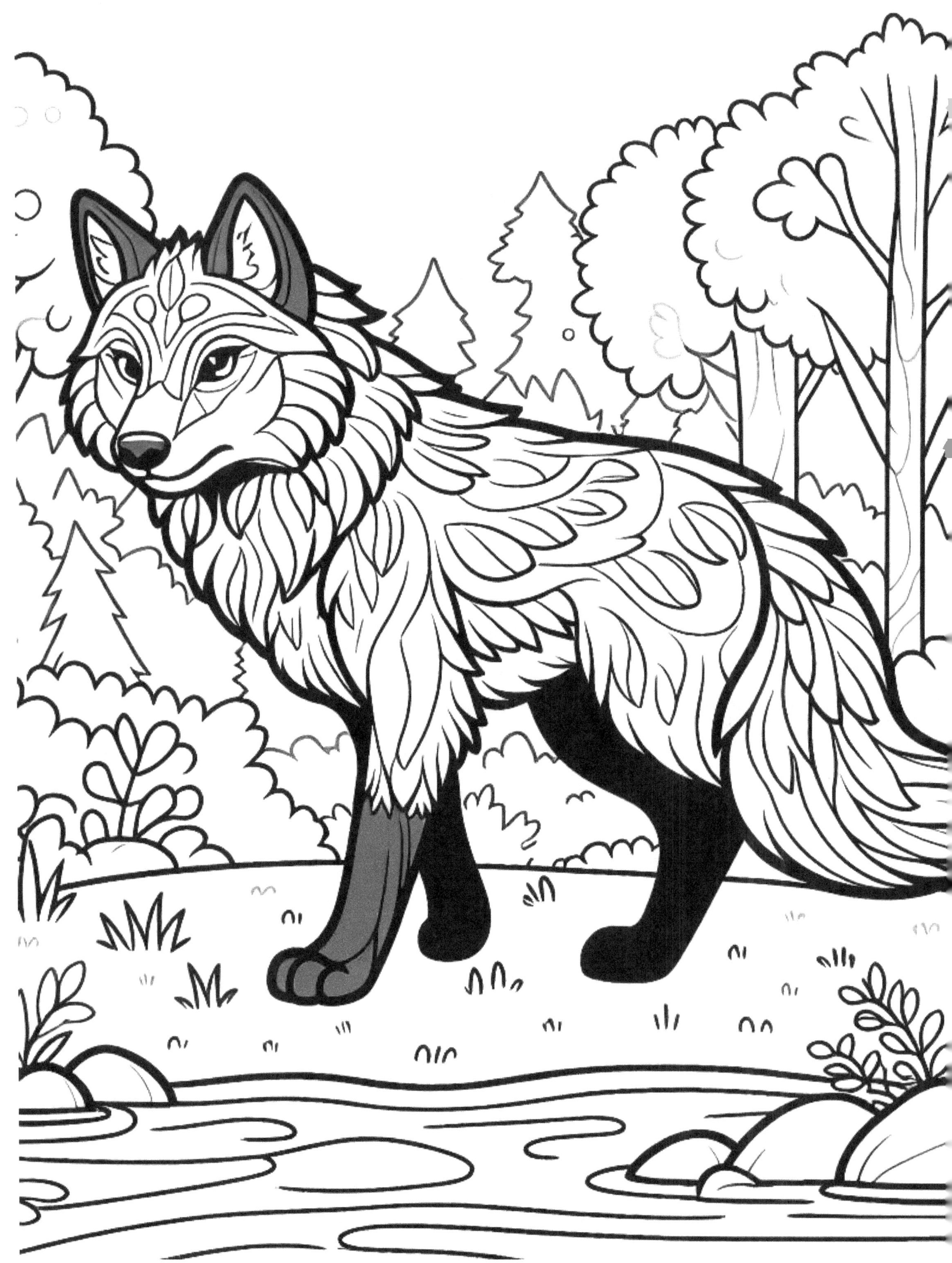

THE RED WOLF

The red wolf (Canis rufus), also known as the eastern red wolf or wood wolf, is a species of canid native to North America.

Why is the red wolf endangered?

The red wolf has been severely affected by habitat loss, hunting, and human persecution. In the early 20th century, it was nearly exterminated across much of its range due to intensive hunting and deforestation. Although conservation and reintroduction efforts have been carried out in some areas, it remains an endangered species and faces significant challenges to its survival.

The red wolf plays an important role in forest ecosystems by regulating prey populations and helping to maintain wildlife balance. Its presence can also have positive effects on forest health by limiting excess herbivory.

In summary, the red wolf is an iconic species of North America that has faced numerous challenges throughout its history. Its conservation is crucial to protect biodiversity and the healthy functioning of forest ecosystems where it inhabits.

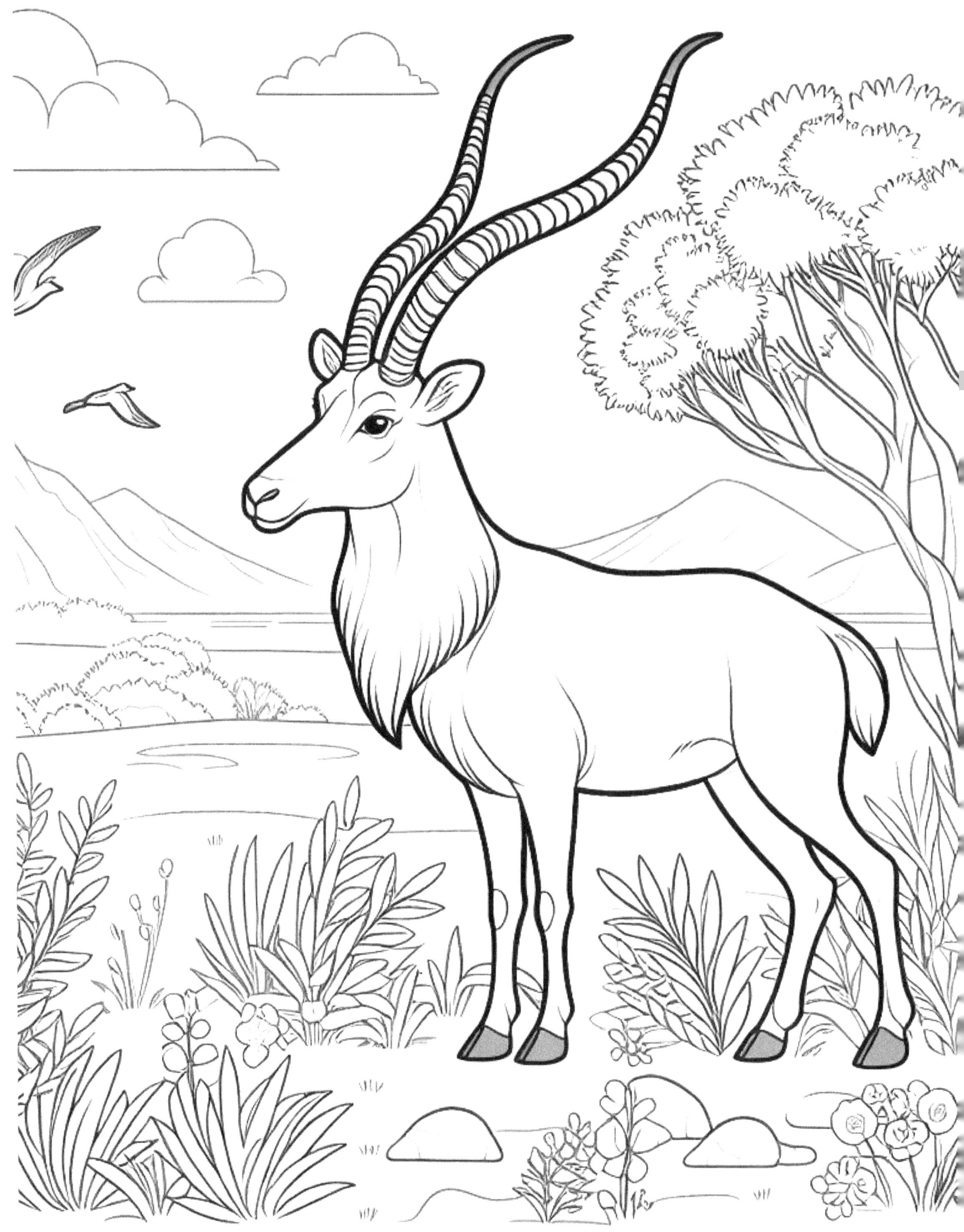

THE SAIGA ANTELOPE

The saiga antelope is a species of antelope that inhabits the steppes and semideserts of Central Eurasia.

Why is the saiga antelope endangered?

The saiga antelope has faced serious threats in recent decades, including poaching for its horns, which are used in traditional Chinese medicine, and habitat loss due to agricultural expansion and urbanization. As a result, the species has experienced a dramatic decline in its population and is classified as critically endangered.

In summary, the saiga antelope is an iconic species of the Eurasian steppes facing serious threats to its survival. Conservation efforts are needed to protect this unique species and restore its populations in the wild.

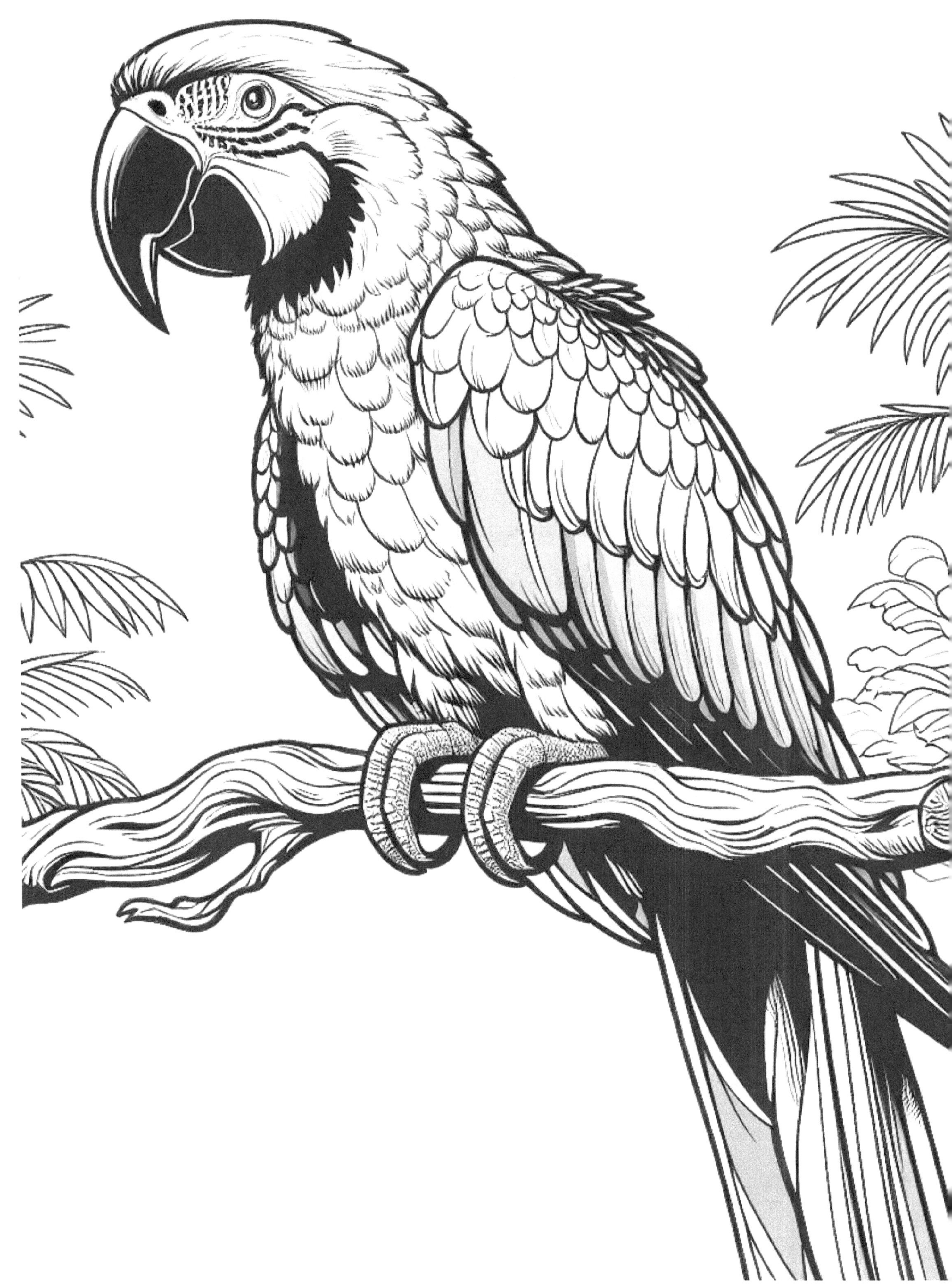

THE SPIX'S MACAW

The Spix's macaw, also known as the Spix's macaw or Little Blue Macaw, is a species of macaw that was endemic to Brazil, specifically the region along the São Francisco River in the northeastern part of the country.

Conservation

The Spix's macaw is classified as extinct in the wild, primarily due to habitat destruction and illegal capture for the pet trade. However, there are captive breeding programs aimed at reintroducing the species into its natural habitat.

In summary, the Spix's macaw is an iconic species that has captured the world's attention due to its beauty and its sad history of extinction in the wild. Conservation efforts are crucial to protect this unique species and restore its presence in the Brazilian environment.

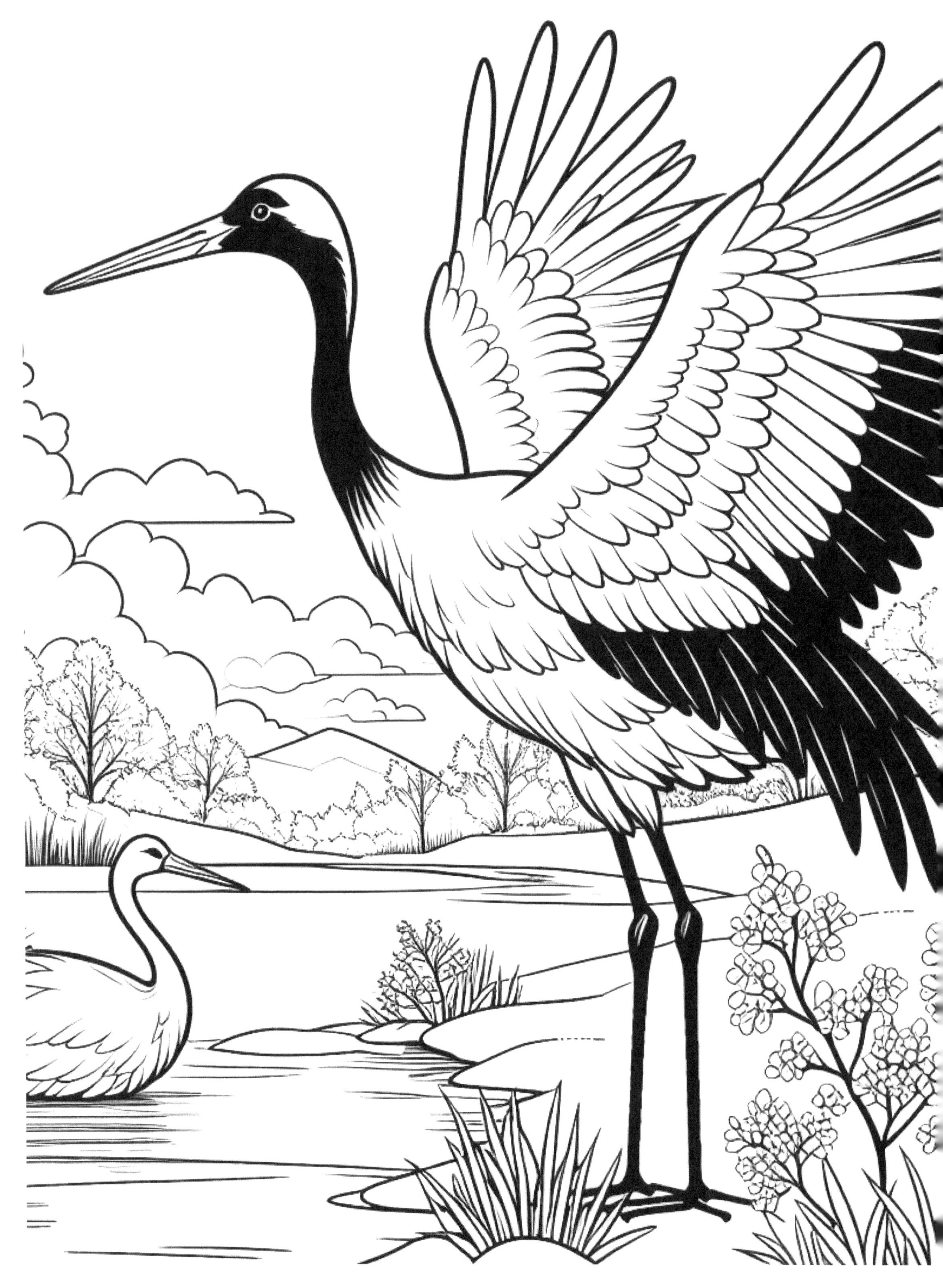

THE SIBERIAN CRANE

The Siberian crane, also known as the white crane, is one of the largest migratory birds in the world and is classified as an endangered species.

Why is the Siberian crane endangered?

The Siberian crane faces numerous threats, including habitat loss due to wetland degradation and water pollution. Illegal hunting and collisions with power lines also pose significant risks to the species. Conservation efforts, such as protecting key habitats and public education on the importance of these birds, are crucial for their survival.

In summary, the Siberian crane is a majestic species that undertakes an epic migration each year. Its conservation is vital for maintaining the health of aquatic ecosystems and ensuring the survival of this iconic species.

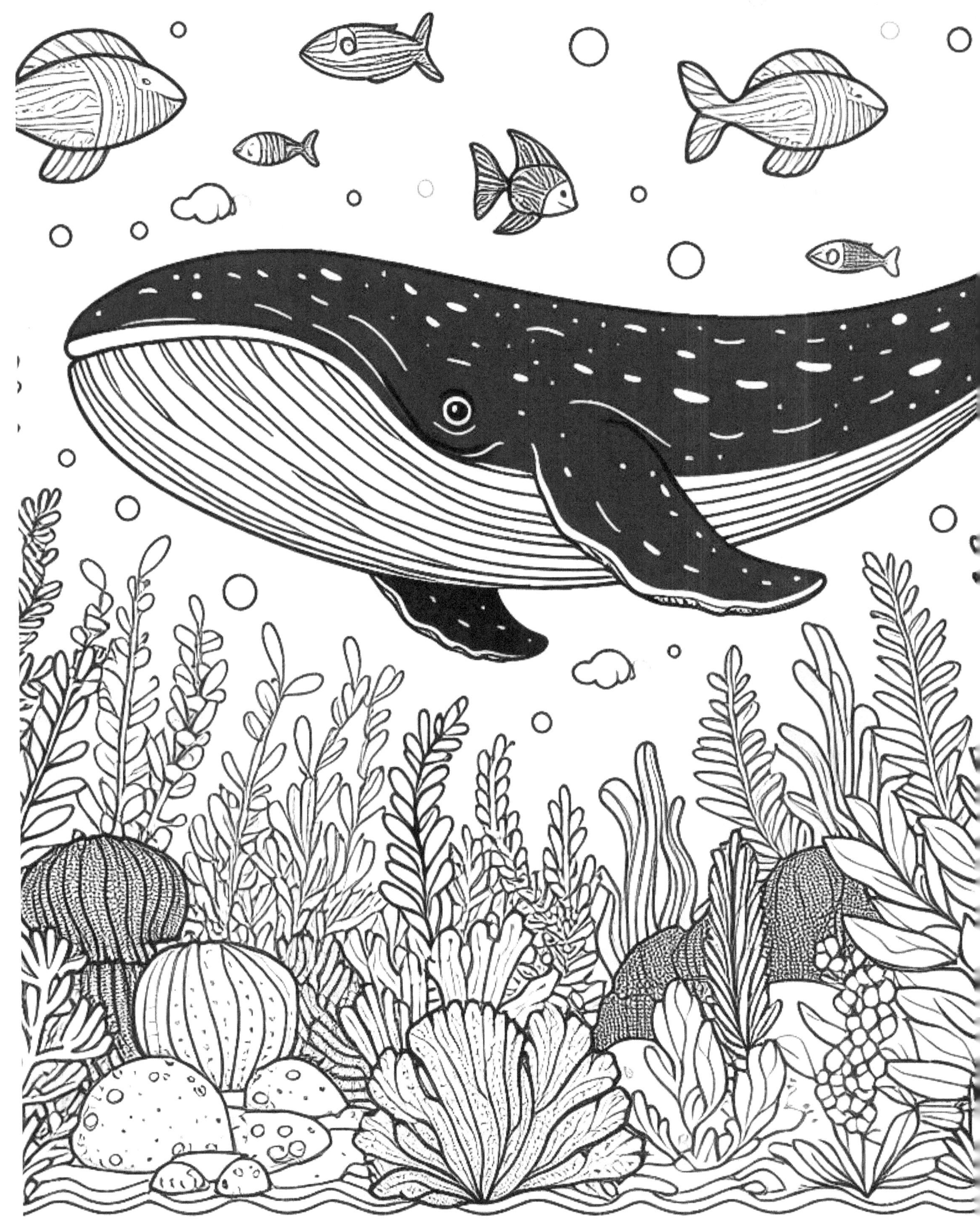

THE BLUE WHALE

The blue whale is the largest mammal on the planet and one of the largest animals to have ever existed on Earth.

Why is the blue whale endangered?

Despite their large size, blue whales have been commercially hunted in the past and still face threats such as ship strikes, acoustic pollution, chemical pollution, and habitat loss due to climate change and marine ecosystem disruption. They are currently classified as an endangered species, and conservation efforts are underway to protect these majestic creatures and their marine habitat.

In summary, the blue whale is an ocean giant that plays a vital role in the marine ecosystem. Their conservation is essential for maintaining the health of the oceans and marine biodiversity worldwide.